SPECIAL OPERATIONS

Air Force Doctrine Document 3-05
16 December 2005

Incorporating Change 2, 28 July 2011

This document complements related discussion found in Joint Publications (JP) 3-0, *Doctrine for Joint Operations*; 3-05, *Doctrine for Joint Special Operations*; 3-05.1, *Joint Special Operations Task Force Operations*; and 3-30, *Command and Control for Joint Air Operations*

Cover Sheet for Air Force Doctrine Document (AFDD) 3-05, *Special Operations*

OPR: LeMay Center/DD

28 July 2011

AFDD numbering has changed to correspond with the joint doctrine publication numbering architecture (the AFDD titles remain unchanged until the doctrine is revised). Any AFDD citations within the documents will list the old AFDD numbers until the doctrine is revised. The changed numbers follow:

OLD	NEW	TITLE
AFDD 2-1	changed to AFDD 3-1	*Air Warfare*
AFDD 2-1.1	changed to AFDD 3-01	*Counterair Operations*
AFDD 2-1.2	changed to AFDD 3-70	*Strategic Attack*
AFDD 2-1.3	changed to AFDD 3-03	*Counterland Operations*
AFDD 2-1.4	changed to AFDD 3-04	*Countersea Operations*
AFDD 2-1.6	changed to AFDD 3-50	*Personnel Recovery Operations*
AFDD 2-1.7	changed to AFDD 3-52	*Airspace Control*
AFDD 2-1.8	changed to AFDD 3-40	*Counter-CBRN*
AFDD 2-1.9	changed to AFDD 3-60	*Targeting*
AFDD 2-10	changed to AFDD 3-27	*Homeland Operations*
AFDD 2-12	changed to AFDD 3-72	*Nuclear Operations*
AFDD 2-2	changed to AFDD 3-14	*Space Operations*
AFDD 2-2.1	changed to AFDD 3-14.1	*Counterspace Operations*
AFDD 2-3	changed to AFDD 3-24	*Irregular Warfare*
AFDD 2-3.1	changed to AFDD 3-22	*Foreign Internal Defense*
AFDD 2-4	changed to AFDD 4-0	*Combat Support*
AFDD 2-4.1	changed to AFDD 3-10	*Force Protection*
AFDD 2-4.2	changed to AFDD 4-02	*Health Services*
AFDD 2-4.4	changed to AFDD 4-11	*Bases, Infrastructure, and Facilities* [Rescinded]
AFDD 2-4.5	changed to AFDD 1-04	*Legal Support*
AFDD 2-5	changed to AFDD 3-13	*Information Operations*
AFDD 2-5.1	changed to AFDD 3-13.1	*Electronic Warfare*
AFDD 2-5.3	changed to AFDD 3-61	*Public Affairs Operations*
AFDD 2-6	changed to AFDD 3-17	*Air Mobility Operations*
AFDD 2-7	changed to AFDD 3-05	*Special Operations*
AFDD 2-8	changed to AFDD 6-0	*Command and Control*
AFDD 2-9	changed to AFDD 2-0	*ISR Operations*
AFDD 2-9.1	changed to AFDD 3-59	*Weather Operations*

BY ORDER OF THE
SECRETARY OF THE AIR FORCE

AIR FORCE DOCTRINE DOCUMENT 3-05
16 DECEMBER 2005
INCORPORATING CHANGE 2, 28 JULY 2011 |

SUMMARY OF CHANGES

Interim change two to Air Force Doctrine Document (AFDD) 2-7 changes the cover to AFDD 3-05, *Special Operations* to reflect revised AFI 10-1301, Air Force Doctrine (9 August 2010). AFDD numbering has changed to correspond with the joint doctrine publication numbering architecture. AFDD titles and content remain unchanged until updated in the next full revision. A margin bar indicates newly revised material.

Supersedes: AFDD 2-7, 16 December 2005
OPR: LeMay Center/DD
Certified by: LeMay Center/DD (Col Todd C. Westhauser)
Pages: 55
Accessibility: Available on the e-publishing website at www.e-publishing.af.mil for
        downloading
Releasability: There are no releasability restrictions on this publication
Approved by: LeMay Center/CC, Maj Gen Thomas K. Andersen, USAF
        Commander, LeMay Center for Doctrine Development
        and Education

FOREWORD

The United States is engaged in a protracted struggle against violent extremists that will persist for the foreseeable future. Our Air Force Special Operations Forces (AFSOF) are at the forefront of this struggle. In recent years, we have called upon AFSOF to deliver unique capabilities and skill sets to combatant commanders across the range of military operations from the major combat operations in Iraq and Afghanistan to the humanitarian relief operations in Haiti.

Air Force Doctrine Document (AFDD) 2–7, Special Operations, guides the preparation and employment of Air Force special operations forces. It builds upon our capstone doctrine, and presents the fundamentals of what Airmen have learned as the best way to organize and employ AFSOF at the operational level of war. AFDD 2–7, *Special Operations*, describes the support AFSOF provides to the joint force commander (JFC) and reiterates the command relationships that allow the JFC to leverage AFSOF capabilities as part of a greater campaign plan.

As we read AFDD 2-7, it is essential we keep the basic SOF truths in mind. AFSOF cannot be mass produced. AFSOF is centered on people and not platforms and therefore quality is always better than quantity. It takes years to produce a strategic SOF Airman. History has demonstrated that we cannot produce competent AFSOF after an emergency arises. Our AFSOF must remain strong and ready to serve. Finally, as we employ AFSOF, All Air Force Airmen must be prepared to enable the AFSOF mission with agile combat support capabilities.

Although proud of our Air Force's successes during our most recent operations, history tells us that we cannot afford complacency. With this in mind, AFDD 2-7 captures lessons learned from latest experiences, adjusts AFSOF's doctrinal sightline, and shapes the foundational concepts to meet current and future challenges.

Norton A. Schwartz
General, USAF
Chief of Staff, United States Air Force

TABLE OF CONTENTS

INTRODUCTION

PURPOSE

This document establishes doctrinal guidance for the employment of Air Force special operations forces across the range of military operations. As the Air Force's keystone document on special operations, AFDD 2-7 provides commanders guidance on organizing AFSOF, and planning and executing Air Force special operations missions.

APPLICATION

This AFDD applies to the Total Force: all Air Force military and civilian personnel, including active, Air Force Reserve Command, and Air National Guard units and members.

The doctrine in this document is authoritative, but not directive. Therefore, commanders should consider the contents of this AFDD and the particular situation when accomplishing their missions. Airmen should read it, discuss it, and practice it.

SCOPE

This publication provides the overarching doctrinal guidance for the conduct of Air Force special operations across the range of military operations. It describes the characteristics, capabilities, United States Special Operations Command (USSOCOM) core activities, Air Force Special Operations Command (AFSOC) core missions, typical organization, and command and control of AFSOF. Furthermore, this publication summarizes support requirements necessary to conduct Air Force special operations missions and defines training and education goals of the United States Air Force Special Operations Forces.

COMAFFOR / JFACC / CFACC
A note on terminology

One of the cornerstones of Air Force doctrine is that "the US Air Force prefers - and in fact, plans and trains - to employ through a commander, Air Force forces (COMAFFOR) who is also dual-hatted as a joint force air component commander (JFACC)." (AFDD 1)

To simplify the use of nomenclature, Air Force doctrine documents will assume the COMAFFOR is dual-hatted as the JFACC unless specifically stated otherwise. The term "COMAFFOR" refers to the Air Force Service component commander while the term "JFACC" refers to the joint component-level operational commander.

While both joint and Air Force doctrine state that one individual will normally be dual-hatted as COMAFFOR and JFACC, the two responsibilities are different, and should be executed through different staffs.

Normally, the COMAFFOR function executes operational control/ administrative control of assigned and attached Air Force forces through a Service A-staff while the JFACC function executes tactical control of joint air component forces through an air operations center (AOC).

When multinational operations are involved, the JFACC becomes a combined force air component commander (CFACC). Likewise, the air operations center, though commonly referred to as an AOC, in joint or combined operations is correctly known as a JAOC or CAOC.

FOUNDATIONAL DOCTRINE STATEMENTS

Foundational doctrine statements are the basic principles and beliefs upon which AFDDs are built. Other information in the AFDDs expands on or supports these statements.

✪ It is highly unlikely special operations would be conducted as a single Service operation; therefore, special operations forces (SOF) planning must consider joint support and coordination. (Page 1)

✪ The most important element of the Air Force's special operations capabilities resides in its aircrews, special tactics teams, combat aviation advisory teams, and support personnel specially trained to conduct a wide array of missions across the range of military operations. (Page 3)

✪ AFSOF are presented to joint force commanders who may organize their forces into functional components. For SOF, this is normally the joint force special operations component commander (JFSOCC). The JFSOCC may establish a joint special operations air component (JSOAC) to exercise OPCON of Joint SOF air. The JSOAC commander is usually dual-hatted as commander of Air Force special operations forces or commander of Army special operations aviation. (Page 6)

✪ All Air Force SOF (AFSOF) based in the continental United States are administratively assigned to Air Force Special Operations Command (AFSOC) and are under the combatant command authority of the commander, United States Special Operations Command. (Pages 17)

✪ The geographic combatant commander normally exercises combatant command (command authority) of all assigned AFSOF and operational control of all attached AFSOF through the commander of the theater special operations command (TSOC). (Page 17)

✪ The TSOC is the primary mechanism by which a geographic combatant commander exercises command and control over SOF. (Page 18)

✪ The joint special operations component commander (JSOACC) is the commander, within a joint special operations component or task force, responsible for planning and executing joint special operations air activities. (Page 19)

✪ AFSOF may be placed under command of a single JSOAC commander in theater, subordinate to the JFSOCC. (Page 20)

✪ The special operation liaison element is a team that represents the JFSOCC to the joint force air component commander (if designated) or appropriate Service component air command and control organization, to coordinate, deconflict, and integrate special operations air, space, cyberspace, surface, and subsurface operations with conventional air, space, and information operations. (Page 20)

✪ Rigorous training and rehearsals of the mission are integral to the conduct of all operations because of the inherent complexity and high risk associated with these missions. (Page 27)

CHAPTER ONE

OVERVIEW OF AIR FORCE
SPECIAL OPERATIONS FORCES (AFSOF)

> *It is the nature of Special Ops that many of your victories are unseen and must remain secret – but I know about them. Our Special Operations Forces are the worst nightmare of America's worst enemies...*
>
> **—President George W. Bush**

INTRODUCTION

This Air Force doctrine document seeks to capture the fundamental principles by which AFSOF guide their actions in support of national objectives. It articulates AFSOF warfighting principles, lessons learned, and best practices for conducting special operations across the range of military operations.

Specifically, this document has three objectives: First, to describe Air Force guidance on the proper use of AFSOF in military operations; second, to explain AFSOF's role in the planning and execution of joint special operations; finally, to analyze AFSOF's unique command relationships that, left unexplained, can introduce confusion and friction in the proper employment of this unique Air Force function. **It is highly unlikely special operations would be conducted as a single Service operation; therefore, SOF planning must consider joint support and coordination.**

As a joint force, SOF are organized, trained, and equipped to accomplish eleven core activities: civil affairs operations, counterinsurgency, counter proliferation of weapons of mass destruction (WMD), counterterrorism, direct action, foreign internal defense, information operations, psychological operations, security force assistance, special reconnaissance, and unconventional warfare.[1] This publication provides an overview of the Airman's perspective of these core activities while other Air Force doctrine documents (AFDDs) discuss some of these tasks in greater detail.[2]

Ultimately, this document reflects best practices, lessons learned, and a conceptual framework that represents the essence of Air Force special operations culture. It is meant to guide and provide a foundation for a commander's professional judgment. With AFSOF doctrine as their point of departure, commanders can adapt to dynamic strategic environments that demand AFSOF involvement in unilateral, joint, multinational, and interagency operations across the range of military operations.

---

[1] USSOCOM Fact Book, http://www.socom.mil/SOCOMHome/newspub/pubs/Documents/FactBook.pdf
[2] For more information, see AFDD 2-3.1, Foreign Internal Defense; AFDD 2-5, Information Operations; AFDD 2-12, *Nuclear Operations;* and AFDD 2-1.8, *Counter CBRNE Operations.* Specific special operations operational guidelines are provided in Joint Publication (JP) 3-05, *Doctrine for Joint Special Operations;* and JP 3-07.1, *Joint Tactics, Techniques, and Procedures for Foreign Internal Defense.*

The Air Force Special Operations Forces Legacy

In preparation for Operation OVERLORD, the cross-channel invasion of France, small numbers of special operations forces began infiltrating Europe as early as 1942. Eventually, the special operators needed their own clandestine air insertion capability. In August 1943, General Carl A. Spaatz, at the time the commander of North African Air Forces, allocated three B-17 bombers to support Office of Strategic Services (OSS) activities. This marked the start of the ever-expanding special air activities in the European theater by specially trained aircrews who came to be known as "Carpetbaggers."

Concurrently, General Henry "Hap" Arnold, commander, Army Air Forces, approved the activation of an American special air unit in the China-Burma-India (CBI) theater of operations. The First Air Commando Group's primary task involved support for Lord Louis Mountbatten's British commando forces in the CBI.

Together, the Carpetbaggers and Air Commandos represent the earliest manifestations of AFSOF. Since World War II, Air Commandos have fought in near-countless conflicts and contingencies. Whether in the Philippines, Korea, Vietnam, Grenada, or Panama, AFSOF have supported United States national objectives honorably and with distinction.

America has always recognized AFSOF value and unique contributions, but in the face of shrinking budgets, America's specialized airpower struggled to remain healthy and viable through peacetime. The American military's inability to adequately respond to the 1979 Iranian hostage crisis highlighted this deficiency within America's SOF community. Although the ill-fated rescue attempt did not make it past its initial landing site--code named DESERT ONE--it ushered in a new era for AFSOF.

Following this failed mission, congressional persistence and support from key leaders within the Department of Defense (DOD) establishment led to the creation of the United States Special Operations Command (USSOCOM) and its Air Force component, the Air Force Special Operations Command (AFSOC).

MODERN AFSOF DEFINED

According to JP 1–02, *DOD Dictionary of Military and Associated Terms*, special operations are: "[o]perations conducted in hostile, denied, or politically sensitive environments to achieve military, diplomatic, informational, and/or economic objectives employing military capabilities for which there is no broad conventional force requirement. These operations often require covert, clandestine, or low-visibility capabilities. Special operations are applicable across the range of military operations.

They can be conducted independently or in conjunction with operations of conventional forces or other government agencies and may include operation through, with, or by indigenous or surrogate forces. Special operations differ from conventional operations in degree of physical and political risk, operational techniques, mode of employment, independence from friendly support, and dependence on detailed operational intelligence and indigenous assets. Also called SO."

Simply put, the term "special operations" is often associated with two types of concepts: Special mission areas and capabilities. Special operations differ from conventional operations in the operational techniques and small size of the friendly force (compared to the enemy), degree of physical and political risk, relative independence from friendly support, mode of employment, reliance on detailed and perishable intelligence, extensive use of indigenous assets, and preference toward detailed planning and rehearsals.

Special operations forces, however, must complement, not compete with nor be a substitute for, conventional forces. The need for an opportunity to attack or engage strategic or operational targets with small units drives the formation of special units with specialized, highly focused capabilities. Although not always decisive on their own, special operations can be designed and conducted to create conditions favorable to US strategic aims and objectives. Often these operations may require clandestine or low visibility capabilities and are applicable across the range of military operations.

After the 1980 failed attempt to rescue US hostages held in Iran, the Air Force organized, trained, and equipped a portion of its force specifically for special operations. As such, AFSOF is an umbrella term for those regular and Reserve Component Air Force forces, designated by Title 10, United States Code, Section 167 or those units or forces that have since been designated as SOF by the Secretary of Defense.

Ultimately, **the most important element of the Air Force's special operations capabilities resides in its aircrews, special tactics teams, combat aviation advisory teams, and support personnel specially trained to conduct a wide array of missions across the range of military operations.** SOF are regionally-oriented, cross-culturally competent,[3] and usually have personnel experienced and conversant in the cultures and languages found in an operational area. SOF elements can provide liaison to facilitate conventional, multinational and interagency interoperability.

Recent successes in toppling the Taliban during Operation ENDURING FREEDOM and unconventional warfare operations in western and northwestern Iraq during Operation IRAQI FREEDOM highlight the complementary nature of conventional and special operations forces. Although the nature of AFSOF operations often demands different tactics than conventional forces, the employment of AFSOF follows the guiding truths that define all air operations, regardless of the functional specialty—the principles of war and the tenets of air and space power.

---

[3] CJCSI 3126.01 *Language and Regional Expertise Planning* 23 Jan 06, page D-9; and USSOCOM Special Operations Language Policy Memorandum 30 March 2009)

AFSOF APPLICATIONS OF THE PRINCIPLES OF WAR

These principles apply to special operations in the same way they apply to conventional operations.

✪ **Objective.** Special operations are best employed in support of a joint force commander's (JFC's) strategic or operational objectives. Many missions are characterized as limited, surgical, physically challenging, low profile, and sometimes separate from the immediate battlefield.

✪ **Offensive.** The lethal application of special operations is inherently offensive in nature because it seeks to strike or engage an adversary to compel or deter his actions. The unique manner of application of SOF offensive capabilities assists JFCs in achieving results that may be unattainable by larger conventional forces.

✪ **Mass.** Special operations concentrate combat power at critical times and in discriminate places to achieve decisive results. Massing combat power while avoiding concentration of forces can enable numerically inferior SOF to achieve decisive results while minimizing both human loss and the misapplication of resources. SOF's ability to strike at key nodes may create results equivalent to those achievable by large force concentrations.

✪ **Economy of Force.** Economy of force is critical to the successful conduct of special operations given the small size and lack of redundant capabilities inherent in special operations tactical units. One way of ensuring economy of force is via an evaluation of proper operational mission criteria. The employment of SOF in support of the joint force campaign or operation plan is facilitated by five basic criteria. These criteria provide guidelines for both conventional and SOF commanders and planners to use when considering the employment of SOF.

1) Is this an appropriate AFSOF mission?

2) Does the mission support the JFC's campaign or operation plan?

3) Is the mission operationally feasible?

4) Are required resources available to execute the mission?

5) Does the expected outcome of the mission justify the risk?

✪ **Maneuver.** AFSOF's capability to maneuver allows them to strike adversaries where and when they are most vulnerable and to avoid their strengths.

✪ **Unity of Command.** Unity of command fosters unity of effort and allows the JFC to integrate and synchronize special operations with every aspect of the campaign. SOF command and control (C2) architecture is often tailored for each mission to achieve this end.

✪ **Security.** Special operations planning and execution require high levels of security integrated fully with operations security (OPSEC) and force protection to protect the nature of these missions.

In addition to the principles of war stated in AFDD 1, the political considerations and the nature of many stability operations require an underpinning of several additional principles:

✪ **Restraint.** Restraint is the application of military force appropriate to the situation. Operating in austere environments, with a small footprint, AFSOF depend on a thorough study of their operating environment to develop a comprehensive understanding of the local culture, the nature of the conflict, and the probable response of the populace. Armed with this understanding, they recognize the likely impact of the use of force and tailor the application of force to the context of the mission.

✪ **Perseverance.** In order to improve the probability of success, special operations, like most conventional capabilities, must be prepared to pursue national goals and objectives patiently, resolutely, and persistently, for as long as necessary to achieve them. For example, AFSOF combat aviation advisors spend years cultivating the desired relationships with allied countries. AFSOF foreign internal defense capabilities, as personified by its combat aviation advisory teams (CAATs), exemplify the protracted application of military capabilities in support of strategic aims.

✪ **Legitimacy.** Generating support at home and among allies is primarily the responsibility of civilian leaders, though military actions must be in line with legitimate goals. AFSOF's inherent cultural and linguistic acumen coupled with a high level of operational skill help to bolster the US military's legitimacy among foreign nations' militaries.

✪ **Surprise.** Because of the sensitive nature of the operations, and the relatively small size of the force, special operations forces rely heavily on the element of surprise. In many cases, operations are conducted clandestinely.

✪ **Simplicity.** The key to successful special operations mission execution lies in the simplicity of the planning. History has demonstrated that as planning increases in complexity, so does the degree of risk.

AFSOF APPLICATIONS OF THE TENETS OF AIR AND SPACE POWER

Every Airman must understand the fundamental guiding truths of air and space power employment—better known as tenets. The tenets of air and space power complement the principles of war. The tenets provide more specific considerations for air and space forces, including AFSOF. As with the principles of war, the tenets require informed judgment in application.

The application of the principles and tenets are left to commanders' judgment as they strive to craft the most effective employment of air and space power for a given situation. The basics of these tenets—centralized control and decentralized execution, flexibility and versatility, synergistic effects, persistence, concentration, priority, and balance—are explained in AFDD 1, *Air Force Basic Doctrine*. The following is a discussion of how they are applied to AFSOF.

Centralized Control and Decentralized Execution

AFSOF are presented to JFCs who may organize their forces into functional components. For SOF, this is normally the joint force special operations component commander (JFSOCC). The JFSOCC may establish a joint special operations air component to exercise OPCON of Joint SOF air. The JSOAC commander is usually dual-hatted as commander of Air Force special operations forces (COMAFSOF) or commander of Army special operations aviation. It is therefore possible for Air Force SOF to be OPCON to an Army aviation commander in his role as JSOAC Commander.

The concept of *decentralized execution* is just as central to the proper application of airpower as centralized control. Delegation of execution authority to responsible, capable lower level commanders is necessary for effective span of control and to foster initiative, situational responsiveness, and tactical flexibility.

Regardless of assigned missions and C2 arrangements, it is critical that AFSOF are integrated into the air tasking order (ATO) and properly adhere to the airspace control order (ACO) to ensure operations are integrated and to prevent fratricide. Real-time coordination between COMAFSOF/JSOACC, COMAFFOR/JFACC, and any other forces operating in the operational environment is vital.

Flexibility and Versatility

AFSOF exemplify the concept of flexibility by being organized, trained, and equipped to achieve a wide variety of missions. For example, during Operation DESERT STORM, AFSOF MH-53J helicopters were part of Task Force Normandy. MH-53s were the pathfinders for Army AH-64 Apache helicopters, ultimately guiding the Apaches to key Iraqi early warning sites. The destruction of these sites enabled the first wave of coalition aircraft to strike targets deep in Iraqi territory, in the first minutes of DESERT STORM. Immediately after they met their objective, the MH-53 crews assumed combat search and rescue duties for the remainder of their mission.

AFSOF versatility is underscored by the fact air commandos can be employed equally effectively at the strategic, operational, and tactical levels. During Operation IRAQI FREEDOM, AFSOF assets assisted in securing Iraqi critical infrastructure, seizing airfields in support of operational campaign objectives, and providing close air support for coalition ground forces, thus producing parallel effects, exemplifying the versatility of air and space power.

Synergistic Effects

The proper application of a coordinated force can produce effects that exceed the contributions of forces employed individually. For instance, AFSOF special tactics teams operating with joint and coalition SOF teams provided terminal attack control and weather support for combat air forces (CAF) during Operations ENDURING FREEDOM and IRAQI FREEDOM.

Persistence

Persistence suggests continued efforts. One example of how AFSOF maintains a global persistent presence across the range of military operations is the employment of combat aviation advisory teams working by, with, and through partner nations to provide coalition interoperability and develop their air and space power.

Concentration

The principles of mass and economy of force deal directly with concentrating the appropriate power at the right time and the right place (or places) to achieve the desired effects. For instance, AFSOF fire support and the infiltration of ground forces were able to concentrate combat power to achieve decisive effects during Operation JUST CAUSE.

Priority

The use of AFSOF assets must account for their limited nature (less than two percent of AF personnel) and the requirement to conserve them for future operations. Demand for AFSOF assets will likely exceed their availability unless commanders establish appropriate priorities.

Balance

Commanders should balance combat opportunity, necessity, effectiveness, efficiency, and the impact on accomplishing assigned objectives against the associated risk to friendly air and space forces. For example, daylight AFSOF operations may offer an attractive alternative to joint force commanders, but the benefit must be balanced against the risk. Depending on the threat, such actions may not be appropriate.

> *In no other professions are the penalties for employing untrained personnel so appalling or irrevocable as in the military.*
>
> **—General Douglas MacArthur**

CHAPTER TWO

CORE ACTIVITIES AND MISSIONS

> *Frederick liked to say that three men behind the enemy were worth fifty in front of him.*
>
> **—Ardant Du Picq**

USSOCOM CORE ACTIVITIESS

SOF conduct eleven special operations core activities.[4] These activities are explained in detail in JP 3-05, *Doctrine for Joint Special Operations*. JP 3-22, *Foreign Internal Defense*, JP 3-24, *Counterinsurgency Operations*, JP 3-26, *Counterterrorism*, JP 3-40, *Combating Weapons of Mass Destruction*, and JP 3-57, *Civil-Military Operations*. As the air component to USSOCOM, AFSOC is responsible to organize, train, and equip AFSOF to provide the necessary air capabilities to conduct or support these activities.

Civil Affairs Operations (CAO): Those military operations conducted by civil affairs forces that: enhance the relationship between military forces and civil authorities in localities where military forces are present; require coordination with other interagency organizations, intergovernmental organizations, nongovernmental organizations, indigenous populations and institutions, and the private sector; and involve application of functional specialty skills that normally are the responsibility of civil government to enhance the conduct of civil-military operations. (JP 1-02)

Counterproliferation of Weapons of Mass Destruction (CP): Actions taken to locate, seize, destroy or capture, recover and render such weapons safe.

Counterterrorism (CT): Actions taken directly against terrorist networks and indirectly to influence and render global and regional environments inhospitable to terrorist networks. (JP 1-02).

Counterinsurgency (COIN): Comprehensive civilian and military efforts taken to defeat an insurgency and to address any core grievances. (JP 1-02).

Direct Action (DA): Short-duration strikes and other small-scale offensive actions conducted as a special operation in hostile, denied, or politically sensitive environments and which employ specialized military capabilities to seize, destroy, capture, exploit, recover, or damage designated targets. Direct action differs from conventional offensive actions in the level of physical and political risk, operational techniques, and the degree of discriminate and precise use of force to achieve specific objectives (JP 1-02).

---

[4] SOCOM Factbook

Foreign Internal Defense (FID): Participation by civilian and military agencies of a government in any of the action programs taken by another government or other designated organization to free and protect its society from subversion, lawlessness, and insurgency (JP 1-02).

Information Operations (IO): The integrated employment of the core capabilities of electronic warfare, computer network operations, psychological operations, military deception, and operations security, in concert with specified supporting and related capabilities, to influence, disrupt, corrupt or usurp adversarial human and automated decision making while protecting our own (JP 1-02).

Information Operations in Recent Conflicts

AFSOF were heavily involved in the IO mission prior to and during the war in Iraq. Getting an early start on the psychological operations (PSYOP) campaign, Air National Guard EC-130 COMMANDO SOLOs began airing "Voice of America" into the Kuwaiti theater of operations on 22 November 1990.

During Operation DESERT STORM the EC-130s targeted defectors by broadcasting "Voice of America'" along with prayers from the Koran and testimony from well-treated prisoners. To convince Iraqi troops to surrender, MC-130 COMBAT TALONS and HC-130 COMBAT SHADOWs dropped some 17 million leaflets over Iraqi defensive positions. The leaflets urged Iraqi soldiers to give up and warned what would happen if they did not. The promise was kept when their positions were either bombed by B-52s or struck by MC-130s dropping BLU-82 (15,000 pound) bombs. This was a model PSYOP campaign, combining information and strike operations. It was extremely effective and caused thousands of Iraqis to flee or surrender.

In Operations ENDURING FREEDOM and IRAQI FREEDOM, COMMANDO SOLO aircraft broadcast hundreds of hours of PSYOP messages. Along with millions of leaflets, dropped mostly by MC-130s, AFSOF were an integral part of the DOD's campaign to shape perceptions. Just as in previous campaigns, these PSYOP messages were tailored to specific audiences. As Secretary of Defense Donald Rumsfeld describes, "We're working to make clear to the Afghan people that we support them, and we're working to free them from the Taliban and their foreign terrorist allies." In all of these operations, AFSOF forces contributed to the commander's objectives through the broadcast and dissemination of PSYOP messages.

Psychological Operations: Planned operations to convey selected information and indicators to foreign audiences to influence their emotions, motives, objective reasoning, and ultimately the behavior of foreign governments, organizations, groups, and individuals. The purpose of psychological operations is to induce or reinforce foreign attitudes and behavior favorable to the originator's objectives (JP 1-02).

Security Force Assistance: The DOD component of Security Force Assistance is the set of activities that contribute to unified action by the US Government to support the development of the capacity and capability of foreign security forces and their supporting institutions. This is an approved USSOCOM core task; however, the definition is in transition. This definition will be included in JP 1-02 upon approval of JP 2-22, Foreign Internal Defense.

Special Reconnaissance (SR): Reconnaissance and surveillance actions conducted as a special operation in hostile, denied, or politically sensitive environments to collect or verify information of strategic or operational significance, employing military capabilities not normally found in conventional forces. These actions provide an additive capability for commanders and supplement other conventional reconnaissance and surveillance actions (JP 1-02).

Unconventional Warfare (UW): A broad spectrum of military and paramilitary operations, normally of long duration, predominantly conducted through, with, or by indigenous or surrogate forces who are organized, trained, equipped, supported, and directed in varying degrees by an external source. It includes, but is not limited to, guerrilla warfare, subversion, sabotage, intelligence activities, and unconventional assisted recovery (JP 1-02).

AFSOC CORE MISSIONS[5]

In order to fulfill the USSOCOM directed tasks explained above, and meet any other tasking as directed by the Secretary of Defense, AFSOF is organized, trained, and equipped to support the following ten core missions:

Agile Combat Support (ACS). Effectively create, prepare, deploy, employ, sustain, and protect Air Force Special Operations Command Airmen, assets, and capabilities throughout the range of military operations at our initiative, speed, and tempo. ACS strives for technological superiority, robustness, agility, and full integration with operations. ACS is the foundational and crosscutting system of support that enables the AFSOC operational mission areas and capabilities of specialized air power: speed, lethality, and global perspective.

Aviation Foreign Internal Defense (AvFID). AvFID operations directly execute US security and foreign policy as lead airpower elements that shape the battlefield and conduct stability operations to enable global reach and strike. This is accomplished by applying the mission set (assess, train, advise and assist foreign aviation forces) across a continuum of operating venues described as indirect assistance, direct assistance (not including combat) and combat operations. Theater security cooperation and

---

[5] AFSOC FY12-37 Master Plan

contingency operation objectives are met through planning and engaging by, with, and through partner nation air forces to enable those forces to participate effectively in security and stability of their nation, thereby reducing the requirement for US airpower resources to remain engaged to ensure stability and security. Activities during indirect and direct assistance include activities that develop capacity and capability to enable foreign airpower. During combat operations the AvFID mission set is applied by assisting foreign airpower to achieve security objectives and integrate foreign air forces into the joint/combined campaign. Execution of the AvFID mission set requires experienced personnel with advanced skills in aviation operations, combined with extensive training and preparation in order to work independently in austere locations while employing foreign aircraft using adaptive tactics, techniques, and procedures.

NOTE: While the AFSOC core mission area is referred to as aviation FID (AvFID), personnel conducting the missions are known as combat aviation advisors (CAA).

Specifically, AFSOF AvFID operations are tailored to assess, train, advise, and assist foreign aviation forces in air operations employment and sustainability. AvFID operations support theater combatant commanders across the range of military operations primarily by facilitating the availability, reliability, safety, interoperability, and integration of friendly and allied aviation forces supporting joint, combined, and multinational forces. AvFID operations provide assistance in the interrelated areas of FID, coalition support (CS), UW, worldwide humanitarian relief/assistance, and disaster relief. AvFID operations also include a liaison role in coalition support. This core mission is expanding. The AFSOF vision is for the coalition support mission to include the current AvFID operations mission, as well as emerging responsibilities within the realm of humanitarian relief /assistance and disaster relief. Here are some of the key duties that CAA are expected to perform:

- Conduct local or regional assessments of foreign aviation forces' capabilities to employ and sustain aviation resources.

- Working through the special operations liaison element (SOLE), CAAs make recommendations to the JFACC regarding capability of foreign aviation units to support combined air operations plan objectives.

- Promote safety and interoperability between US forces and coalition partners.

- Act as an air and space power force multiplier by developing and executing tailored training programs to increase the tactical effectiveness of HN aviation resources in support of the combatant commander's objectives.

- Facilitate area air defense coordination and airspace deconfliction via the AOC.

- Provide assistance to aviation forces in direct participation of FID, CS, UW, humanitarian relief/assistance, and disaster relief.

✪ Provide liaison to JFACC, through the SOLE, to coordinate, harmonize and integrate foreign aviation forces supporting multinational air operations.

For more information on FID, see AFDD 2-3.1, *Foreign Internal Defense.*

Battlefield Air Operations (BAO). BAO is a unique set of combat proven capabilities (combat control, pararescue, special operations weather, and tactical air control party) provided by regular and Air Force reserve component SOF battlefield Airmen who integrate, synchronize, and control air and space assets (manned and unmanned) to achieve tactical, operational and strategic objectives. These capabilities include, but are not limited to, air traffic control; assault zone assessment, establishment, and control; joint terminal attack control (JTAC); fire support operations; operational preparation of the environment; special reconnaissance, including terminal and en route observations, environmental collection and prediction, weather forecasting, and mission analysis for weather impacts on operations; command and control communications; full spectrum personnel and equipment recovery; and battlefield trauma care.

Command and Control. The exercise of authority and direction by a properly designated commander over assigned and attached forces in the accomplishment of the mission. Command and control functions are performed through an arrangement of personnel, equipment, communications, facilities, and procedures employed by a commander in planning, directing, coordinating, and controlling forces and operations in the accomplishment of joint/combined special operations.

Information Operations. Information operations are the integrated employment of the capabilities of influence operations, electronic warfare operations, and network warfare operations, in concert with specified integrated control enablers, to influence, disrupt, corrupt, or usurp adversarial human and automated decision making while protecting our own. Information operations provide predominantly nonkinetic capabilities to the warfighter. These capabilities can create effects across the operational environment and are conducted across the range of military operations. Information superiority is a degree of dominance in the information domain that allows friendly forces the ability to collect, control, exploit, and defend information without effective opposition. Information superiority is a critical part of air, space and cyberspace superiority, which gives the commander freedom from attack, freedom to maneuver, and freedom to attack. Information operations are integral to all AFSOC operations and may support, or be supported by, air, space, ground, and cyberspace operations. IO, therefore, must be integrated into air, space, and cyberspace component operations in the same manner as traditional air and space capabilities. The thorough integration of kinetic and nonkinetic air, space, cyberspace, and information capabilities provides the Air Force with a comprehensive set of tools to meet military threats.

Information operations conducted at the operational and tactical levels may be capable of creating effects at the strategic level and may require coordination with other national agencies. While the AFSOF community often has to compartmentalize actions due to the nature of its missions, in particular with regards to IO, AFSOF must ensure that its IO initiatives support the JFC's campaign plan. AFSOF may leverage any of the three IO capabilities—influence operations, electronic warfare operations, and network warfare operations. The following are some examples of how AFSOF can achieve IO effects:

✪ By delivering IO messages (e.g., via leaflets), or delivering the SOF operators who will convey the IO message (e.g., infiltration of land/sea SOF) in order to influence a variety of audiences.

✪ By using electronic warfare to degrade or disrupt enemy communications and weapon systems, thereby enhancing survivability.

✪ By leveraging deception via network warfare operations in order to hide intention from enemy collection systems.

Intelligence, Surveillance, and Reconnaissance (ISR). Synchronize and integrate platforms and sensors for the planning and direction; collection; processing and exploitation, analysis and production and dissemination process. These activities provide actionable intelligence, weather, environmental awareness and prediction across all SOF command echelons from force to unit level. ISR provides the operational environment awareness necessary to plan and conduct kinetic and non-kinetic operations and includes all the associate organization, equipment, and training.

Precision Aerospace Fires.[6] Provide combatant commanders with an integrated capability to find, fix, track, target, engage, and assess (known in USSOCOM as find, fix, finish) targets using a single weapons system or a combination of systems. Execute close air support, air interdiction, and armed reconnaissance missions with required persistence, connectivity, situational awareness, and target identification, lethality, and survivability in low- to selected high-threat operational environments.

Psychological Operations. Planned operations to convey selected information and indicators to foreign audiences to influence their emotions, motives, objective reasoning, and ultimately the behavior of foreign governments, organizations, groups, and individuals. The purpose of psychological operations is to induce or reinforce foreign attitudes and behavior favorable to the originator's objectives. AFSOC supports PSYOP dissemination by providing both aerial dissemination of radio / television PSYOP products and aerial delivery of leaflets.

Specialized Air Mobility (SAM). The conduct of rapid, global infiltration, exfiltration, and resupply of personnel, equipment, and materiel using specialized systems and tactics. These missions may be clandestine, low visibility, or overt and through hostile, denied, or politically sensitive airspace using manned or unmanned platforms.

---

[6] AFSOC usage retains the term "aerospace" in describing its core missions and so it is retained here. Nevertheless, this term has been generally superseded in doctrinal usage, since "airpower," as both a concept and a set of capabilities, is now understood to encompass the integrated use of air, space, and cyberspace - the domains in and through which the Air Force preeminently exercises power and influence.

The AFSOF mobility mission area includes the rapid global airlift of personnel and equipment through hostile airspace to conduct operations and to enable air mobility across the range of military operation. AFSOF are an integral part of the Air Force team and provide unique capability to the JFC, JFACC, and JFSOCC. AFSOF deployment readiness and unique training contribute to their constant readiness status and to their ability to quickly respond. They often are the first forces to deploy on a global scale. AFSOF capabilities accommodate all operational and physical environments—especially conditions of adverse weather, darkness, and denied territory. Operations may be conducted with a single aircraft or as part of a larger force package and are normally conducted during one period of darkness.

AFSOF's contribution to rapid global mobility is not limited to aircraft but includes the key ground role played by special tactics teams (STTs). While not a formal element of the global air mobility support system (GAMSS), STTs play an integral part in rapid global mobility. They are the dynamic link between the surface forces and the air assets that deliver, sustain, and recover them. An Air Force objective performed by AFSOF is to rapidly respond to developing situations, obtain an early assessment and prevent escalation by presence or support to the rapid deployment of right-sized follow-on forces.

STTs are uniquely trained and equipped to rapidly deploy and conduct airfield assessment and airfield surveys in austere and hostile environments. STTs are the Air Force's initial provider of tactical airfield navigational/approach systems and terminal air traffic control (ATC) services. To this end, STTs maintain the capability to perform airfield selection, evaluation, survey, and establishment, including en route and terminal navigation aids (for example, mobile microwave landing system [MMLS] and portable tactical air navigation [TACAN]), ATC, and terminal control of close air support for air base defense.

In addition to "first there" ATC and airfield management, STTs also perform these functions for landing zones (LZs) and drop zones (DZs). As the airhead matures, STTs hand off these tasks for sustained operations to other elements. STT make it possible for theater forces, air and space expeditionary task forces (AETFs), and lead mobility wings to seamlessly deploy and employ.

The following are examples of how AFSOF support rapid global mobility and global attack expressed in terms of air and space power functions:

✪ Providing limited self-deployment.

✪ Tailoring deployment and employment support of forces to, from, and within the operational environment.

✪ Providing long-range infiltration, exfiltration, and resupply of forces in hostile and denied territory.

- Supporting AETF deployment with airlift aircraft and crews trained and equipped for self-protection.

- Supporting AETF deployment with STTs.

- Selecting, evaluating, surveying, and establishing airfields including en route and terminal navigation aids (MMLS and TACAN) for joint / coalition forces.

Key to AFSOF mobility is the ability of rigorously trained AFSOF aircrews to successfully penetrate hostile airspace using specially designed aircraft. With penetrating capability, however, comes the limitation of the size of the force and materiel that AFSOF aircraft can deliver. Select conventional airlift forces who habitually train with SOF can augment the joint special operations air component, and integrate with AFSOF to provide a more robust specialized mobility capability.

Specialized Refueling. The conduct of rapid, global refueling using specialized systems and tactics. This includes aerial refueling of vertical lift aircraft and ground refueling during forward arming and refueling point operations. These missions may be clandestine, low visibility, or overt and in hostile, denied, or politically sensitive environments using manned or unmanned platforms by the following methods:

- Providing air refuelable vertical lift and fixed-wing aircraft, thereby greatly increasing flexibility and range.

- Providing forward arming refueling points which have the ability to refuel and arm vertical lift and fixed-wing assets at unimproved airfields.

- Augmenting conventional rescue units with refueling assets.

Service Core Functions

One of twelve Air Force Service core functions (SCFs), derived through the Quadrennial Roles and Missions Review process, is special operations. The special operations SCF works in cooperation with the other core functions to provide our nation with Global Vigilance, Reach, and Power in the pursuit of national objectives. While these SCFs are not doctrine, per se, they provide a terminological bridge between the language used by the operational community (as found in this and other doctrine) and the language used by the [force acquisition] planning, programming, and budgeting (PPB) community, to help relate missions accomplished in actual contingencies and operations to capabilities developed by PPB processes.

Special operations supports and is supported by all of the other Air Force core functions. It supports our joint and Service doctrine and joint operations concepts by providing capabilities that are tailored specifically to special operations and bolster coalition and joint operations.

Special operations Service core functions (SCF) "mission areas," AFSOC "core missions," and USSOCCOM "core activities" are compatible and broadly consistent, but are not phrased identically, due to different language requirements and terminology conventions between the AFSOF operational community, the PPB community within the Air Force that defines the SCFs, and USSOCCOM's differing joint terminological standards. Regardless of differences in usage, however, the basic sets of capabilities and missions can be correlated across AFSOC operational, Air Force PPB, and USSOCCOM force presentation and command contexts.

CHAPTER THREE

COMMAND, CONTROL, AND ORGANIZATION

> *Special operators fight a different kind of war. A war that often involves more training of other forces than fighting. A war that frequently requires observation rather than attack. A war that pits a handful of special operators against large conventional forces. A war that is most likely to take place during "peacetime," before and after military conflict, in an attempt to prevent crises or put things back together if war is unavoidable.*
>
> **—Susan Marquis,**
> ***Unconventional Warfare: Rebuilding U.S. Special Operations Forces***

COMMAND RELATIONSHIPS

Assignment of Air Force Special Operations Forces

In the continental United States (CONUS): Unless otherwise directed by the Secretary of Defense, **all AFSOF based in the CONUS are administratively assigned to AFSOC and are under the combatant command authority of the commander, USSOCOM.** USSOCOM is a unique command in the Department of Defense in that it has the responsibilities of a functional combatant command, has Service-like responsibilities in areas unique to special operations and, when established as a supported command, plans and conducts certain special operations missions worldwide. CDRUSSOCOM exercises combatant command authority (COCOM) over assigned SOF through the commanders of its Service components or its subordinate unified command.

Outside of CONUS: AFSOF assigned to a geographic combatant command are under the COCOM of the respective geographic combatant commander. **The geographic combatant commander normally exercises COCOM of all assigned AFSOF and operational control (OPCON) of all attached AFSOF through the commander of the TSOC.** For conventional missions, the JFACC may receive OPCON or TACON of AFSOF assets when directed by the JFC. However, in most cases, AFSOF will only be in a direct support relationship with conventional assets. Therefore, C2 should remain through special operations channels.

AFSOC, the parent command and lead proponent for AFSOF, normally retains some portion of administrative control (ADCON) of all active duty AFSOF personnel. Under less than full mobilization, AFSOC shares ADCON with Air Force Reserve Command of all deployed reserve AFSOF personnel. AFSOC, however, may elect to share ADCON with other Air Force major commands. For example, via current memoranda of agreement, AFSOC shares ADCON with Pacific Air Forces and United States Air Forces Europe.

Regardless of the arranged command relationship, commanders should:

✪ Provide for a clear and unambiguous chain of command.

✪ Avoid frequent transfer of AFSOF between commanders.

✪ Provide for sufficient staff experience and expertise to plan, conduct, and support the operations.

✪ Integrate AFSOF in the planning process.

✪ Match unit capabilities with mission requirements.

COMMAND, CONTROL, AND ORGANIZATION

Presentation of Forces

Like other Air Force units, AFSOF forces are presented at the direction of Secretary of Defense to the component commanders. Although AFSOF habitually serve two masters with regards to force management—the Air Force and USSOCOM—AFSOF assets are presented to the JFC via SOF channels. Therefore, whether through USSOCOM or the TSOC, requests for forces are sourced through special operations and not Air Force channels.

Command and Control of AFSOF in Theater

Theater Special Operations Command. To provide the necessary unity of command, each geographic combatant commander (except for US Northern Command, which has a special operations division) has established a TSOC as a subunified command within the geographic combatant command. **The TSOC is the primary mechanism by which a geographic combatant commander exercises command and control over SOF** (see Figure 3.1).

Joint Special Operations Task Force (JSOTF). A JSOTF is a JTF composed of special operations units from more than one Service, formed to carry out specific special operations or prosecute special operations in support of a theater campaign or other operations. A JSOTF may have conventional non-special operations units assigned or attached to support the conduct of specific missions. A notional depiction of JSOTF elements is shown in Figure 3.2. The JSOTF is an interim entity, designed to perform a specific mission. According to JP 3-05.1, *Joint Tactics, Techniques, and Procedures for Joint Special Operations Task Force Operations*, "once it is established and a commander, joint special operations task force (COMJSOTF) is designated, a decision process occurs to organize and tailor the JSOTF to accomplish the mission."

18

Joint Forces Special Operations Component Commander (JFSOCC). The JFSOCC is the special operations functional component commander within a unified command, subunified command, or JTF responsible to the establishing commander for making recommendations on the proper employment of assigned, attached, or made available for tasking SOF and assets; planning and coordinating special operations; or accomplishing such operational missions as may be assigned. This is a more permanent arrangement than the JSOTF. In fact, the TSOC commander will normally be established as a JFSOCC if there is more than one JSOTF to command (see Figure 3.1.). If only one JSOTF is established (e.g., within a JTF), the commander, JSOTF (CDRJSOTF) will be dual-hatted as the JFSOCC. Normally, the JFC exercises OPCON of AFSOF through the JFSOCC.

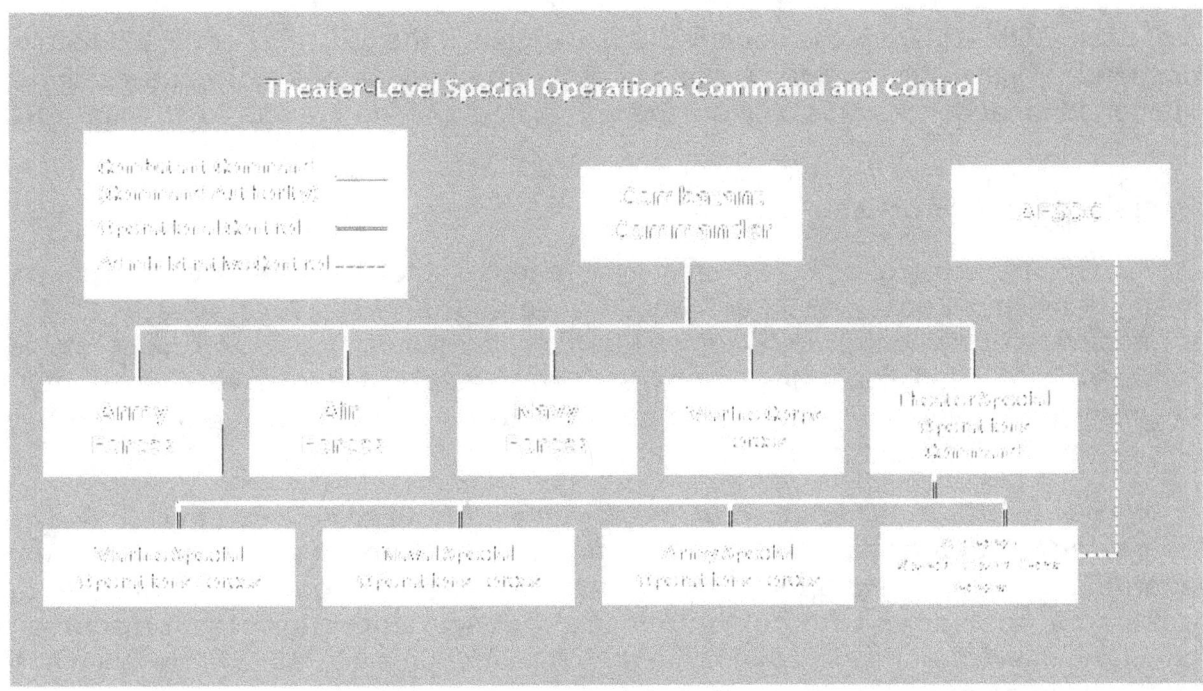

Figure 3.1. Special Operations Forces

Joint Special Operations Air Component. A JFSOCC or CDRJSOTF may establish a JSOAC. The JSOAC is established as a functional component within a joint special operations force (TSOC, JFSOC, of JSOTF) to control special operations aviation assets. **The joint special operations air component commander (JSOACC) is the commander, within a joint special operations component or task force, responsible for planning and executing joint special operations air activities.** This includes the responsibility to coordinate, allocate, task, control, and support the assigned joint special operations aviation assets, to include unmanned aircraft systems and other assets tasked to support special operations. The JFSOCC or CDRJSOTF normally delegates OPCON of joint special operations aviation to the JSOACC.

The JSOAC, established by the JFSOCC, may support a single JSOTF or multiple JSOTFs within the theater. Regardless of the number of supported elements, the ability of specialized airpower to range on a theater and global scale imposes theater and global responsibilities that can be discharged only through the integrating function of centralized control under an Airman. To preserve unity of command and enable the most effective use of limited special operations aviation assets, **AFSOF may be placed under command of a single joint special operations air component commander (JSOACC) in theater, subordinate to the JFSOCC.** For example, in situations where multiple JSOTFs are established and the JSOAC is a theater-wide organization, the JSOACC should be subordinate to the JFSOCC, not any one JSOTF commander (see Figure 3.2). Figure 3.3 depicts a scenario when only one JSOTF exists in theater and the JSOACC might be subordinate to the JSOTF commander..

Commander Air Force Special Operations Forces

The COMAFSOF is the senior AFSOF Airman in the JFSOCC or JSOTF chain of command. Within this construct, there is only one person clearly in charge; for the superior commander, there is only one person to deal with on matters regarding AFSOF issues.

Special Operations Liaison Element

SOF are most effective when fully integrated into the overall campaign plan. Liaison between all components of the joint force and SOF, wherever assigned, is vital for effective employment of SOF as well as the prevention of fratricide. The element that performs this function at the combined air operations center (CAOC) is the SOLE. The mission of the SOLE is to act as a liaison to the JFACC or appropriate Service component air C2 organization.

The SOLE is a team that represents the JFSOCC to the JFACC (if designated) or appropriate Service component air C2 organization, to coordinate, deconflict, and integrate special operations air, space, cyberspace, surface, and subsurface operations with conventional air, space, and information operations. The SOLE director works directly for the JFSOCC and provides a SOF presence in the CAOC, is aware of SOF activities in the field, and provides visibility of SOF operations in the ATO and the ACO. Additionally the SOLE coordinates appropriate fire support coordinating measures to help avoid fratricide. Although not an all-inclusive list, the SOLE provides the following functions:

✪ Harmonizes JFSOCC strategy and targets with JFACC's intent and vision via liaison with the strategy division.

✪ Injects all SOF requirements (to include Army and Naval SOF contingent) within the JFACC's master air attack plan via close coordination with the JFACC's combat plans division.

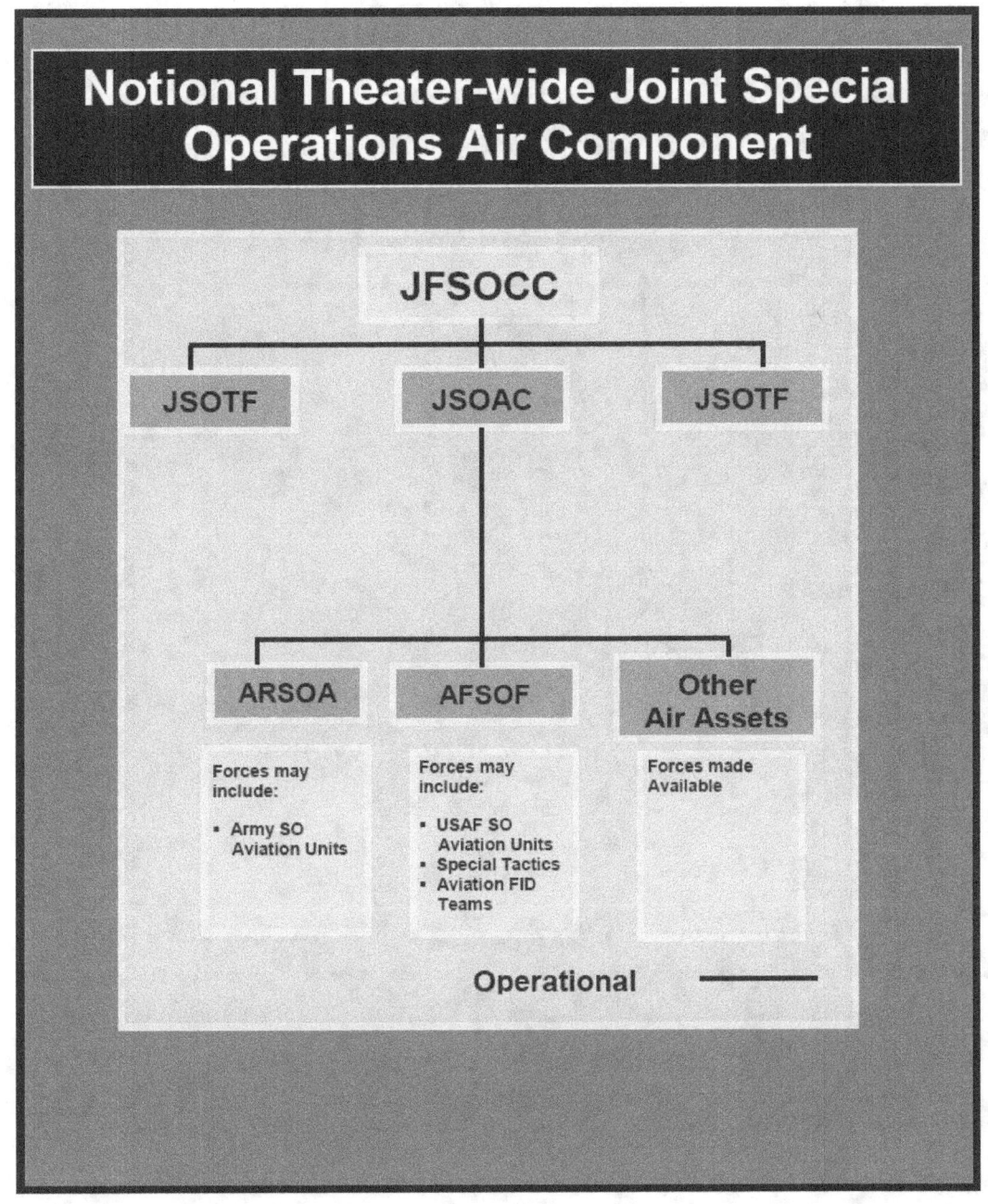

Figure 3.2. Notional Theater-wide Joint Special Operations Air Component (JSOAC)

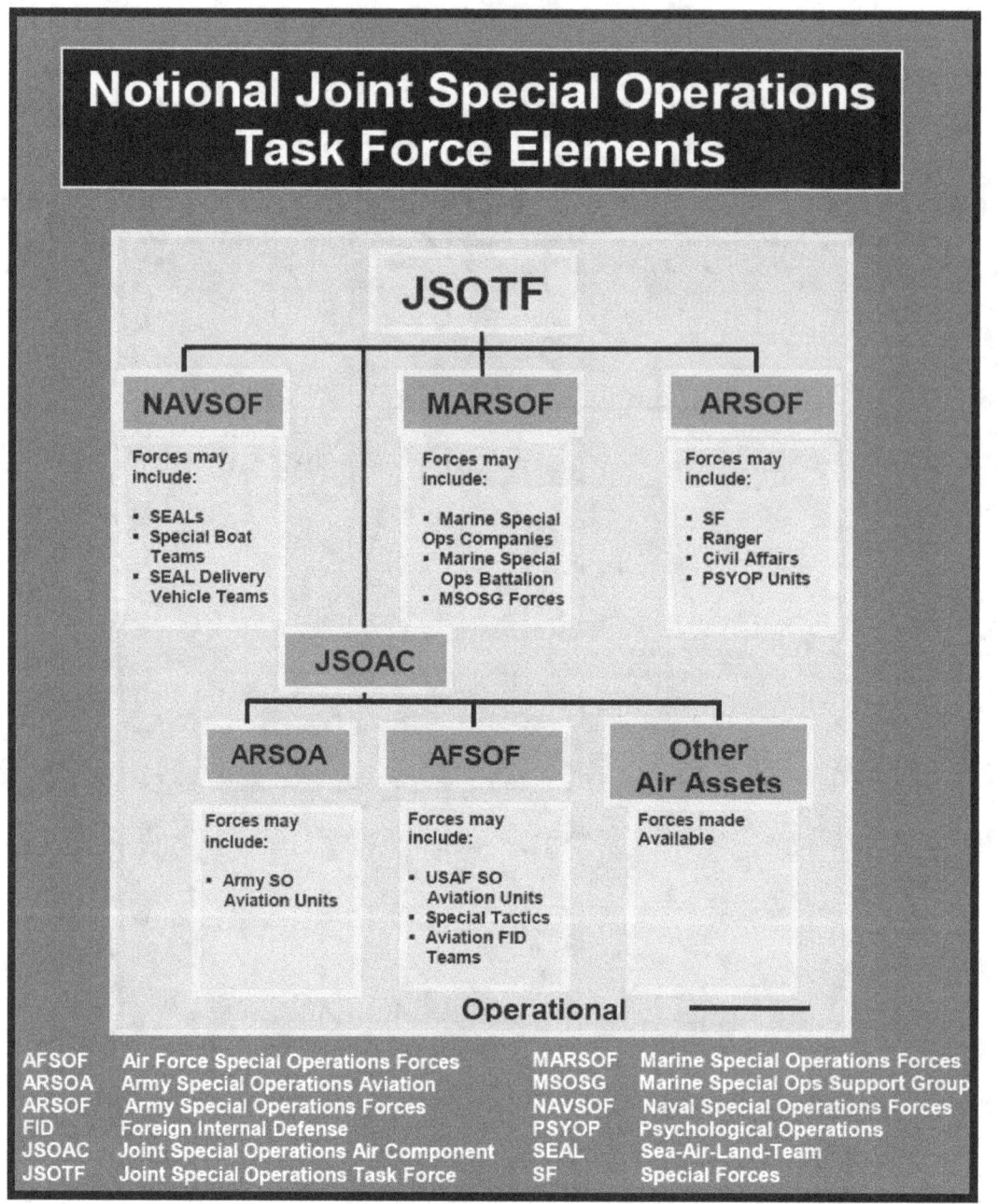

Figure 3.3. Notional Joint Special Operations Task Force Elements

○ With coordination with the combat plans division, facilitates all JFSOCC inputs into the ACO, ATO, and Special Instructions (SPINS). In essence, the SOLE provides for sufficient staff experience and expertise to plan, monitor, and support the operations.

○ Provides updates for situational awareness to the JFACC's combat operations division in order to coordinate close air support (CAS) and request immediate support for time-sensitive targets.

- Monitors and deconflicts SOF activities and locations to prevent fratricide.

- Coordinates real-time ISR requirements for the JFSOCC.

- Synchronizes SOF personnel recovery activities with the joint personnel recovery center (JPRC).

- Coordinates SOF component space requirements with the JFACC when the JFACC is designated the space coordinating authority (SCA).

- Coordinates and monitors SOF support of conventional units and operations (e.g., AC-130 Gunships conducting CAS in support of non-SOF units).

- Provides additional deconfliction between SOF and other aircraft to include unmanned aircraft during theater air operations.

JFACC Support to SOF

SOF missions routinely require JFACC support. For example, the JFACC reduces risk to SOF mission success by providing air superiority in the joint special operations area (JSOA). By gaining and maintaining freedom of movement/freedom from attack, the JFACC provides an umbrella of protection that facilitates and enables the success of SOF missions. This support requires detailed integration and is normally coordinated by the SOLE. Creating and maintaining habitual relationships with the JFACC best facilitate this integration. When conventional forces are tasked to support SOF performing JFSOCC missions, C2 of conventional forces requiring detailed integration or participation in SOF missions should be exercised by the JSOACC if he has the C2 capability. Otherwise, the COMAFFOR/JFACC will exercise C2 of conventional forces and coordinate with the JFSOCC/ JSOTF/JSOACC.

Another notable example of support to SOF, regardless of the enemy air threat, is the JFACC's CAS to ground SOF elements. Operations ENDURING FREEDOM and IRAQI FREEDOM are peppered with examples of JFACC-provided CAS to special tactics and special forces teams engaged in firefights with Taliban, Al Qaeda, or Iraqi forces.

SOF Support to the JFACC

Reciprocating JFACC support to SOF missions, the special operations component may have to likewise support or enable JFACC tasking and priorities. Historical documentation of SOF exploits during Operations ENDURING FREEDOM and IRAQI FREEDOM offer a more detailed example of SOF support to the JFACC.

In Afghanistan and Iraq, AFSOF special tactics teams leveraged air and space power by providing accurate targeting and weather data that enabled the dismantling of the Taliban and Saddam Hussein war machines.

Organization of Expeditionary Air Force Special Operations Forces

AFSOF, like all Air Force units, fit under the AETF construct. Due to its unique relationship with USSOCOM, AFSOF provides deployed unit designations that differ slightly from the conventional Air Force model. Although the names differ, AFSOF organizational patterns are quite similar to conventional unit orientation and functionality.

During Operation ENDURING FREEDOM, AFSOF STT members assisted anti-Taliban Forces in Afghanistan. STTs and JTACs coordinated CAS that enabled the fall of the Taliban with a minimum commitment of US and coalition ground forces.

AFSOC Historical Data

Expeditionary Special Operations Wing (ESOW). An ESOW normally is composed of the wing command element and several groups. ESOWs will carry the numerical designation of the wing providing the command element. Deployed assigned or attached groups and squadrons will retain their numerical designation and acquire the "expeditionary" designation. AFSOF presented as an ESOW will be given with OPCON to the geographic combatant commander, who will normally exercise that authority through the TSOC or JFC via the JFSOCC. In turn, the JFSOCC will normally delegate OPCON to the JSOACC. The Commander, Air Force Special Operations Command will retain some ADCON authorities.

Expeditionary Special Operations Group (ESOG). An ESOG is composed of a slice of the wing command element and some squadrons. Since Air Force groups are organized without significant staff support, a wing slice is needed to provide the command and control for ESOGs smaller than the normal wing. AFSOF ESOGs will be given with OPCON to the GCC, who will normally exercise that authority through the TSOC or JFC via the JFSOCC. In turn, the JFSOCC will normally delegate OPCON to the JSOACC. The Commander, Air Force Special Operations Command will retain some ADCON authorities.

Expeditionary Special Operations Squadron (ESOS) and Expeditionary Special Tactics Squadron (ESTS). The squadron is the basic fighting unit of the Air Force. The ESTS is the basic administrative and logistics support unit enabling multiple STTs and individual operators augmenting other coalition forces.

Expeditionary Elements below Squadron Level. In addition to expeditionary wings, groups, and squadrons, the Air Force can deploy elements below the squadron level for specific, limited functions. These include individuals and specialty teams such as STTs, CAAT, and combat support. They may deploy independently of other Air

Force units, often to remote locations, and may operate directly with other Services. For ADCON purposes, these elements should normally be retained by AFSOC or delegated to the forward deployed COMAFSOF. Examples of such deployed elements might augment a joint psychological operations task force (JPOTF) or an STT supporting a contingency response group (CRG).

CHAPTER FOUR

AFSOF PLANNING AND SUPPORT CONSIDERATIONS

> *...special operations forces succeed, in spite of their numerical inferiority, when they are able to gain relative superiority through the use of a simple plan, carefully concealed, repeatedly and realistically rehearsed, and executed with surprise, speed, and purpose.*
>
> **—William H. McRaven,**
> ***Spec Op: Case Studies in Special Operations Warfare***

GENERAL

Historically, AFSOF tasking has ranged from missions that called specifically for the unique capabilities that AFSOF provides the combatant commander to undertakings that were tasked because AFSOF was the only force that could accommodate the tasking due to time constraints or mission location. Regardless of how or why the tasking reached the AFSOF doorstep, past, present, and future air commandos must provide a candid assessment of AFSOF capabilities, limitations, and risks associated with the mission to the tasking commander.

AFSOF missions are often high-risk/high-payoff operations, have limited windows of execution, and require first-time success. Given the limited size and sustainability of AFSOF, adequate support is vital to the success of the mission and must be properly planned. Additionally, mission rehearsal is a key critical element of mission preparation. This chapter offers some planning considerations when preparing for the employment of AFSOF elements in combat.

MISSION PREPARATION CONSIDERATIONS

Mission Rehearsal

Rehearsal of special operations is critical. Often, repeated rehearsal of certain mission elements is necessary. This is because both personnel and essential tasks differ from mission to mission and because of the possible strategic implications of these missions. Because special operations are unique, each operation may bring together a group of specialists who have worked together infrequently or

Repeated and realistic dress rehearsals make success more certain.

never at all. In addition, the specific tasks required for success may not have been practiced together or integrated in the required sequence. Through rehearsal, a plan's flaws are discovered, and its options are tested. Rehearsals help reduce the risk to SO mission success by revealing plan shortfalls. **Rigorous training and rehearsals of the mission are integral to the conduct of all operations because of the inherent complexity and high risk associated with these missions.** The requirement for a rehearsal can present challenges when operating with the JFACC's forces since the JFACC normally operates on a 72-hour ATO planning cycle.

MAYAGUEZ INCIDENT

On 12 May 1975, the USS *Mayaguez*, an American-owned freighter, was boarded and seized by Cambodian forces while in international waters off the coast of Cambodia. The next day, the ship was taken to Koh Tang Island while the ship's crew was taken to another island for interrogation. The operation to take back the ship and rescue the crew highlights what can happen if reaction time is short, force selection is ad hoc, previous joint training is not done, and mission rehearsal cannot occur in the time available.

The plan called for 11 Air Force helicopters (six HH-53 Air Rescue Service and five CH-53 special operations helicopters) to support Marines in an assault on Koh Tang Island and to board and retake the *Mayaguez* itself. It was assumed that the ship's crew was being held on Koh Tang Island and the rescue force was told to expect only a handful of lightly armed Khmer Rouge soldiers.

The operation began on the morning of 15 May 1975. Retaking the *Mayaguez* went smoothly. The operation at Koh Tang Island, however, soon deteriorated into what one helicopter pilot described as "absolute and utter chaos." As it turned out, there were about 300 Khmer Rouge dug in on the island with heavy weaponry. By the time the first assault was completed, all but one of the original assault helicopters had been destroyed or damaged. Ironically, about three hours into the first assault, the Cambodians gave the entire crew of the *Mayaguez* back to forces from the USS *Holt*; the original problem had been solved. The Marines on Koh Tang Island, however, had to be reinforced and then extracted. These operations lasted through the night. In the end, US casualties were 15 killed in action, three missing in action, and about 49 wounded in action.

—A Very Short War, John F. Guilmartin

Note: This rescue special operation highlights points made elsewhere in this document. Intelligence is key to special operations--all source intelligence must be readily available and regularly exercised by special operations planners. Joint teams conducting special operations must train together regularly and do detailed mission rehearsals to be effective. When deciding how quickly to act, planners must weigh the advantages of further preparation against the advantages of a quick reaction. Finally, operations against foes of uncertain strength must include armed escort in the force package.

Air Force losses for this operation included 23 Airmen, 5 flight crew and 18 Security Police from the 56th Security Police Squadron, lost in a helicopter crash before the personnel were able to participate in the operation.

Cultural, Regional and Linguistic Context[7]

AFSOF is facing an expanding and dynamic operational environment that requires the ability to operate in and across the gamut of cultural, regional and linguistic contexts. Understanding the changing operational environment is critical to the success of AFSOF core missions. Cross-cultural competence and foreign language proficiency are force multipliers that increase efficiency and lower risks to its core missions. Therefore, select AFSOF personnel require the ability to negotiate, communicate and relate to members of our joint and interagency teams, coalition partners and potential adversaries. To achieve this ability, these select personnel need targeted language and cultural competence education and training, and all personnel need cross-cultural competence education and training to appropriately, effectively and decisively achieve desired effects. The type and level of training should be appropriate to the individual's position, function and career path. Commanders must plan and optimize cultural, regional and language training requirements to provide the most significant training in the most effective manner.

OPERATIONAL PLANNING CONSIDERATIONS

Security

OPSEC, communications security (COMSEC) and physical security are vitally important to AFSOF. From initial planning stages to the force recovery stages of a special operation, mission-critical information and OPSEC indicators should be tightly controlled to prevent the adversary from deriving or collecting information that would compromise the mission success. AFSOF habitually operates from secure training sites and employment bases, in order to shield the small, tailored AFSOF from the attention of hostile intelligence collectors. Since AFSOF have little organic base defense capability, they depend almost exclusively on conventional Air Force units or sister Service support for perimeter security.

Additionally, AFSOF pay particular attention to COMSEC, in order to control inadvertent release of mission-critical information and OPSEC indicators. For example, AFSOF maximize secure communications that ensure communication discipline (emissions control) and discretion (low probabilities of detection and intercept). Effective planning and coordinating can ensure information is adequately controlled, while ensuring access to information, equipment, and activities necessary for flexible yet compartmented operations.

Intelligence

In past warfare, a lower level of effort was required to identify the enemy (an armored division massed on the border); however, in today's conflicts, a greater level of effort is required to identify the enemy (terrorist networks, cells, and leadership). Therefore, AFSOF planning and execution are intelligence-intensive, timely, and

---

[7] CJCSI 3126.01 *Language and Regional Expertise Planning* 23 January 2006, and USSOCOM Special Operations Language Policy Memorandum 30 March 2009

detailed. Tailored, all-source intelligence is vital in support of AFSOF. All-source intelligence should be broad in scope, yet adequately detailed. Due to the nature of special operations tasking, AFSOF intelligence specialists must be prepared to provide information on a broad spectrum of target sets associated with the eleven specific core activities explained in Chapter 2.

In essence, intelligence requirements for AFSOF are similar to those of other air components, though the degree of detail is frequently greater. Also, the nature of the objective may require different, tailored support. For instance, AFSOF may need intelligence to avoid enemy forces, where other forces may wish to engage those forces. AFSOF normally attempts to avoid detection for two reasons: It is a requirement on clandestine missions, and it is a method to avoid engagement on any mission. Therefore, detailed intelligence and mission planning are key elements of AFSOF adequate preparation. Some of the products often associated with AFSOF mission planning are:

✪ SOF mission folders.

✪ Mission planning orders validated through rehearsal(s).

✪ Evasion plan of action for all missions.

✪ Combat tactics and concepts of employment based on expected threat scenarios.

✪ Target materials.

✪ Annotated Imagery.

✪ Specialized geospatial products.

Release of post-mission reports with organically collected intelligence, target area analysis, and intelligence assessments may be constrained by the sensitivity of many types of SOF missions. Depending on the sensitivity of the mission, commanders should report data either through special access or routine intelligence reporting channels, as appropriate. To the extent possible, sensitive information may be provided when sources and methods are removed (e.g. tear line).

Communications

AFSOF communications consist of three broad categories: C2, mission support, and tactical communications. Communications for C2 deal with operational planning and execution, which require immediate and responsive communications connectivity from the JFC and JFSOCC through the JSOAC to the most forward deployed SOF forces. Command and control communications must enable AFSOF operators to rapidly deploy and dynamically operate on a global scale with assured connectivity and security in all environments. Tactical communications are carried by SOF airborne and supporting or supported ground forces to communicate with command stations and other SOF elements in operational missions. Interoperability between tactical communications and C2 networks is critical. Low probability of detection and low probability of interception are critical requirements for SOF tactical communications means. AFSOF requires integral communications resources that are characterized by high reliability, flexibility, light weight, and a small footprint. SOF initial and on-the-move communications must be rapidly and continuously available to operate in a variety of threat environments. Man-packable equipment must be operational within minutes versus hours or days. AFSOF communications forces contain, and normally require, organic communications specialists and equipment to provide these rapidly deployable communications capabilities. SOF combat support communications provides deployed network infrastructure, secure telecommunications services, and access to the global information grid (GIG). Access to the GIG enables planning, intelligence, logistics, and other functions at austere deployed operating locations. Mission support communications infrastructure may be provided on a limited basis by SOF unit deployable communications teams or by host base operating support. SOF deployable communications teams are trained and equipped to provide specialized and general communications services for initial AFSOF beddown support. They are intended to move forward to austere operating locations with AFSOF aviation units.

Operational Risk Management (ORM)

By minimizing unnecessary loss of personnel, equipment, and materiel to mishaps, commanders preserve combat capability. Safety staffs identify, evaluate, and recommend corrective actions for hazards associated with employing weapon systems and satisfying operational and training requirements. "First-in, last-out" safety professional presence fosters a hazard identification/risk management mindset can assist commanders, functional managers, supervisors, and operators in the reduction of risks and hazards. This approach is consistent with mission requirements and the principles of ORM:

✪ Accept no unnecessary risk.

✪ Make risk decisions at the appropriate level.

✪ Accept risk when benefits outweigh the costs.

✪ Integrate ORM into operations and planning at all levels.

For more on this, refer to AFI 90-901, *Operational Risk Management*.

Space Operations

AFSOF relies on space capabilities and assets to enable combat operations. To accomplish this, AFSOF requires timely, accurate, and current space products and support during all phases of special operations from initial planning through deployment and execution. To ensure the proper integration of space capabilities, space personnel are assigned to AFSOF units and are task organized into the AFSOC Space Support Team (SST) to support contingency operations. The AFSOC deploys SSTs as part of the SOLE and AFSOF C2-nodes to include the JSOAC, JSOAD, and Air Force special operations detachment as required. As the AFSOF space experts, these teams plan and coordinate the necessary SOF space requirements through the SCA, normally the JFACC, in order to ensure cross-component space tasking consolidation, prioritization, and deconfliction.

Military Deception

Commanders and operations planners must consider incorporating military deception into battle plans and individual missions from the beginning of the planning process to support combat objectives and to enhance the overall probability of mission success. Early implementation is the key to deception success. In many cases the groundwork can be started before SOF arrive in theater. Military deception helps a commander maintain operational security and achieve surprise by causing an adversary to misallocate combat, combat support, or intelligence resources in time, place, or quantity. Military deception planning processes parallel and complement the normal sequence of operations planning actions, therefore military deception planners should be involved in all phases of execution planning.

We need a greater ability to deal with guerilla forces, insurrection, and subversion...We must be ready now to deal with any size force, including small externally supported bands of men; and we must help train local forces to be equally effective.

—President John F. Kennedy, Message to Congress, 1961

Training

AFSOF place extraordinary demands on personnel. Demanding tasks require knowledgeable, trained individuals. Most AFSOF weapon systems and their associated training requirements are unique within the Air Force. To ensure combat readiness, AFSOF are trained to meet their most demanding standards. AFSOF training is constant in order to maintain proficiency at complex special operations core activities. To complement training, AFSOF use mission planning and rehearsal devices to enhance survivability and mission effectiveness.

AGILE COMBAT SUPPORT REQUIREMENTS

Agile combat support consists of those functions necessary to support and sustain operations at a base. The majority of these functions are not organic to AFSOF and therefore must be provided by the COMAFFOR or other service component commander tasked with providing such support. The COMAFFOR, through an air expeditionary wing (AEW) or air expeditionary group (AEG) commander, is normally responsible for providing the combat support and Service common logistics support required by deployed AFSOF. At forward operating locations where the preponderance of forces are AFSOF, the AFSOF commander is responsible for ensuring combat support and Service common logistics support are provided at that location.

The AFSOF commander should coordinate Air Force Service support requirements directly through the COMAFFOR's A-staff. Other support requirements may be provided by a service component commander other than COMAFFOR, per the geographic combatant commander's direction. SOF unique support requirements should be coordinated via SOF channels. Because AFSOF must often deploy and be operational early in the initial phase of any operation, sufficient combat support capability must be planned and deployed on a rapid enough timeline to achieve sustained operational capability, with minimal risk, commensurate with the geographic combatant commander's operational objectives.

Logistics

AFSOF should provide sustainment requirements to the Air Force component logisticians during both contingency and crisis action planning. Coordination of the AFSOF logistics support concept with the Air Force component logisticians and early identification of requirements are key to responsive sustainment support. Provision of Service common logistics support and SOF unique logistics support should be seamless to deployed AFSOF using a single Air Force supply chain and the joint theater distribution system.

AFSOF must be able to execute time sensitive, discrete deployments. A reduced deployed logistics footprint can enhance both the timely response and the security of an operation. The system used to mobilize and deploy AFSOF should be able to function in an environment where OPSEC precludes normal predeployment coordination. However, planners must balance the need for OPSEC against the need for adequate logistics support and the size of the logistics footprint to ensure timely deployment and, ultimately, mission success. Lack of adequate logistics support can put the mission as much at risk as the failure to maintain appropriate OPSEC.

AFSOF normally require logistics support from conventional forces.

Because AFSOF generally operate small numbers of highly specialized aircraft, they should be adequately supported by readiness spares packages (RSP). The RSPs should be maintained at sufficient levels to ensure a quick response and sustained operating capability for short duration contingencies.

Special Operations Weather

AFSOF weather teams provide environmental data collection operations and indigenous personnel weather liaison/training in the deep battle space as well as tailored environmental products for unique worldwide missions of both conventional and special operations forces. The JFSOCC, in coordination with the JFSOCC staff weather officer, determines the correct mix of weather resources required on the ground to support JFC objectives. AFSOF units, such as STTs, have enhanced performance when accompanied by an organic weather capability in the form of a special operations weather team (SOWT). Team composition is scenario-dependent and generally consists of forward observing, planning and mission execution forecasting, and staff weather services. SOWT members are able to independently operate in permissive and semi-permissive environments or as an attachment to SOF teams in hostile areas. SOWT are the only force in the DOD organized, trained, and equipped to perform special reconnaissance operations in support of environmental requirements for the JFC.

While other forces have the ability to provide basic weather reporting, SOWTs can immediately apply their collection efforts to the JFC's mission. SOWTs can perform these tasks while employed tactically on or near the target, along flight routes, or from forward staging areas. In coordination with the JFSOCC staff weather officer, AFSOF weather forces develop an environmental sensing strategy that supports the theater sensing strategy. Deployed special operations weather forces are normally attached with specification of OPCON to a JFSOCC. ADCON support is normally provided by COMAFSOF. SOWTs contain specially trained personnel who deploy to collect and furnish weather information in hostile/denied areas. SOWTs record and transmit timely, accurate, and operationally focused forward-area weather observations for supporting SOF and conventional missions. The environmental information collected by SOWTs should be rapidly relayed to higher-echelon weather agencies and integrated into global and theater computer forecast models for inclusion in operational decision-making processes.

Legal

Planning and execution of Air Force and joint special operations will raise many significant legal issues, including law of armed conflict, use of force, fiscal law, environmental law, international agreements, and other legal considerations. The key to avoiding legal obstacles to mission accomplishment is early identification and resolution of potential legal issues before they become "show stoppers." Active involvement by SOF-knowledgeable judge advocates, providing legal advice to commanders, planners, and operators, must be sought and used from the earliest stages of planning throughout mission execution. Commanders must ensure that qualified legal support is integrated into mission planning, rules of engagement development and publication, aircrew and operator training, and actual mission execution across the full range of military operations.

Medical

AFSOF medical support requirements depend on the number of supported personnel, their locations, the military situation, and access to existing medical facilities. AFSOF missions often test the limits of personal endurance. AFSOF personnel often operate from areas where the lack of preventive medicine measures during mission planning and early phases of execution could result in mission degradation. In addition to rendering routine or emergency medical care to deployed personnel, AFSOF medical personnel should be able to ensure applicable elementary field sanitation and hygiene, disease prevention and control, and environmental risk factor assessment and control. AFSOF aerospace physiology team supports high altitude airdrop missions and human performance threat assessments.

AFSOF medical personnel provide detailed analysis for planning and intelligence functions. They should be aware of potential health hazards, endemic diseases, and other related data associated with the destination country. Plans and procedures also ensure medical personnel comply with the combatant commander's directed deployment surveillance criteria.

Recovery of hostages or survivors normally presents unique medical considerations for those who have been subjected to traumatic events. Hostages or survivors may be confused, apprehensive, physically incapacitated, or act in a manner that can impede their rescue. SOF personnel conducting personnel recovery missions should also be prepared to use indigenous medical facilities to support hostage recovery operations.

AFSOF medical personnel establish the SOF casualty care continuum. They are responsible for planning and conducting medical care from the point of injury back to forward resuscitative surgical care. AFSOF medical and pararescue personnel are charged with providing initial stabilization in personnel recovery and mass casualty incidents.

AFSOF provide organic evacuation to points where conventional airlift and aeromedical evacuation (AE) are located. To support this requirement, selected AFSOF operational medical personnel train on SOF fixed and rotary wing aircraft to provide casualty evacuation from the point of injury back to a conventional interface point. AFSOF medical planning should address ground-air evacuation interface, organic resources to provide pre-evacuation stabilization, transload tactics, and hand-off procedures with conventional medical and AE forces.

Since AFSOC medical assets are limited, commanders should carefully consider available resources when assigning AFSOC medical personnel casualty evacuation roles and other contingency tasking forward of the AFSOC force bed-down location. Sound risk management processes must be considered when determining the best resource to provide this capability. Appropriate planning and tailoring of force size during the predeployment planning phases will greatly assist in ensuring availability of the required medical resources to meet operational requirements. AFSOC medical assets are designed for rapid deployment and to deploy for short durations.

AFSOC has developed medical modules that can be deployed incrementally or totally in the multiples required to support operational requirements. Medical personnel receive extensive medical training and AFSOC medical equipment and supply packages are designed to be highly mobile, relatively lightweight, and sufficient to provide a total spectrum of medical care in austere environments. AFSOC medical modules can serve as the stand-alone medical capability or the initial building blocks to which additional medical assets may be added. These additional assets may be acquired from AFSOC, other Services SOF medical elements, or from conventional military medical assets. Use with other AFSOC units and other medical units gives AFSOC the capability of providing a robust medical presence.

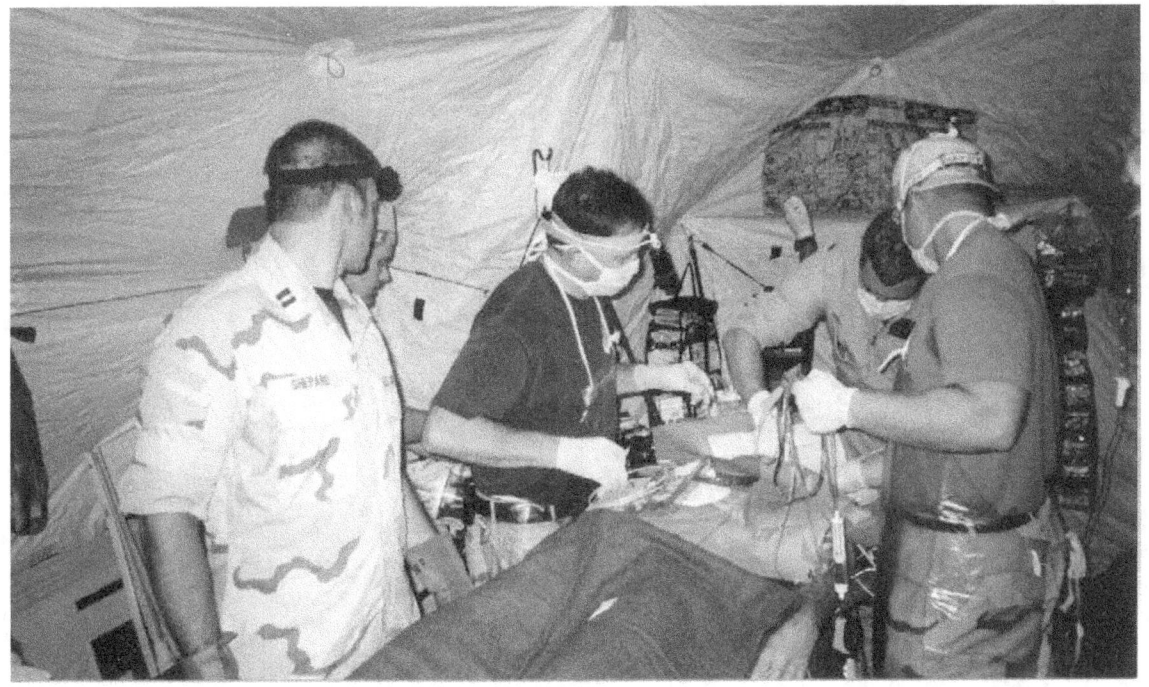

At the Very Heart of Warfare Lies Doctrine. . .

SUGGESTED READINGS

Air Force Publications (Note: All Air Force doctrine documents are available on the LeMay Center web page at **https://wwwmil.maxwell.af.mil/au/lemay/**)

AFDD 2-3, *Irregular Warfare*

AFDD 2-3.1, *Foreign Internal Defense*

AFDD 2-5, *Information Operations*

AFDD 2-12, *Nuclear Operations*

AFDD 2-1.8, *Counter- CBRN Operations*

AFSOC FY 12-37, Master Plan

Joint Publications

CJCSI 3126.01 *Language and Regional Expertise Planning*

JP 3–0, *Joint Operations*

JP 3–05, *Doctrine for Joint Special Operations*

JP 3–05.1, *Joint Tactics, Techniques, and Procedures for Joint Special Operations Task Force Operations*

JP 3-13, *Joint Doctrine for Information Operations*

JP 3-24, *Counterinsurgency Operations*

JP 3–30, *Command and Control for Joint Air Operations*

United States Special Operations Command, *USSOCOM SOF Reference Manual*

USSOCOM Special Operations Language Policy Memorandum, 30 March 2009

Other Publications

Adkin, Mark, *Urgent Fury: The Battle for Grenada.* (Lexington: Lexington Books). 1989.

Beckwith, Charlie A., *Delta Force.* (San Diego: Harcourt Brace Jovanovich). 1983.

Bidwell, Shelford, *The Chindit War: Stillwell, Wingate, and the Campaign in Burma: 1944.* (New York: Macmillan). 1979.

Boykin, William G., *The Origins of the United States Special Operations Command.* (Carlisle Barracks: Army War College). 1992.

Chinnery, Philip D., *Any Time, Any Place: Fifty Years of the USAF Air Commando and Special Operations Forces, 1944-1994.* (Annapolis: Naval Institute Press). 1994.

Guilmartin, John F., *A Very Short War: The* Mayaguez *and the Battle of Koh Tang.* (College Station: Texas University Press). 1995.

Haas, Michael E., *Apollo's Warriors, USAF Special Operations during the Cold War.* (Maxwell AFB: Air University Press). 1997.

Kelly, Orr, *From a Dark Sky.* (Novato: Presidio Press). 1996.

Kyle, James H., *The Guts to Try.* (New York: Orion Books). 1990.

McConnell, Malcolm, *Just Cause: The Real Story of America's High-Tech Invasion of Panama.* (New York: St. Martin's Press). 1991.

McRaven, William H., *Spec Ops: Case Studies in Special Operations Warfare: Theory and Practice.* (Novato: Presidio Press). 1995.

Parnell, Ben, *Carpetbaggers: America's Secret War in Europe.* (Austin: Eakin Press). 1987.

Ryan, Paul B., *The Iranian Rescue Mission: Why It Failed.* (Annapolis: Naval Institute Press). 1985

Schemmer, Benjamin, *The Raid.* (New York: Harper & Row). 1976.

Stubbs, Richard, *Hearts and Minds in Guerrilla Warfare.* (New York: Oxford Press). 1989.

Vandenbrouke, Lucien, *Perilous Options.* (New York: Oxford Union Press). 1993.

Waller, Douglas C., *The Commandos.* (New York: Simon and Schuster). 1994.

GLOSSARY

Abbreviations and Acronyms

ACO	airspace control order
ACS	agile combat support
ADCON	administrative command
AE	aeromedical evacuation
AEG	Air Expeditionary Group
AETF	air and space expeditionary task force
AEW	Air Expeditionary Wing
AFDD	Air Force doctrine document
AFSOC	Air Force Special Operations Command
AFSOF	Air Force special operations forces
AOC	air and space operations center
ATC	air traffic control
ATO	air tasking order
AvFID	aviation foreign internal defense
BAO	battlefield air operations
C2	command and control
CAA	combat aviation advisory
CAAT	combat aviation advisory team
CAF	combat air forces
CAOC	combined air operations center
CAS	close air support
CBI	China/Burma/India
CDRJSOTF	commander, joint special operations task force
CDRUSSOCOM	Commander, United States Special Operations Command
CMO	civil-military operations
COCOM	combatant command (command authority)
COMAFFOR	commander, Air Force forces
COMAFSOF	commander Air Force special operations forces
COMJSOTF	commander, joint special operations task force
COMSEC	communications security
CONPLAN	concept plan
CONUS	continental United States
CP	counterproliferation
CRG	contingency response group
CS	coalition support
CT	counterterrorism
DA	direct action
DZ	drop zone

ESOG	expeditionary special operations group
ESOS	expeditionary special operations squadron
ESOW	expeditionary special operations wing
ESTS	expeditionary special tactics squadron
FID	foreign internal defense
GAMSS	Global Air Mobility Support System
GIG	global information grid
IO	information operations
ISR	intelligence, surveillance and reconnaissance
JFACC	joint force air component commander
JFC	joint force commander
JFSOCC	joint force special operations component commander
JP	joint publication
JPOTF	joint psychological operations task force
JPRC	joint personnel recovery center
JSOA	joint special operations area
JSOAC	joint special operations air component
JSOACC	joint special operations air component commander
JSOTF	joint special operations task force
JTF	joint task force
JTAC	joint terminal attack controller
LZ	landing zone
MMLS	mobile microwave landing system
OPCON	operational control
OPSEC	operations security
OPLAN	operational plans
ORM	operational risk management
OSS	Office of Strategic Services
PSYOP	psychological operations
RSP	readiness spares package
SAM	specialized air mobility
SCA	space coordinating authority
SOF	special operations forces
SOLE	special operations liaison element

SOWT	special operations weather team
SPINS	special instructions
SR	special reconnaissance
SST	space support team
STT	special tactics team
TACON	tactical control
TSOC	theater special operations command
USSOCOM	United States Special Operations Command
UW	unconventional warfare
WMD	weapons of mass destruction

Definitions

Air Force special operations forces. Those active and reserve component Air Force forces designated by the Secretary of Defense that are specifically organized, trained, and equipped to conduct and support special operations. Also called **AFSOF.** (JP 1-02)

Aviation Foreign Internal Defense. Programs for assessing, training, advising, assisting and equipping host nation aviation forces in the sustainment, employment, and integration of airpower to support their internal defense and development programs. Also called **Av FID** (AFDD 2-7)

clandestine operation. An operation sponsored or conducted by governmental departments or agencies in such a way as to assure secrecy or concealment. A clandestine operation differs from a covert operation in that emphasis is placed on concealment of the operation rather than on concealment of identity of sponsor. In special operations, an activity may be both covert and clandestine and may focus equally on operational considerations and intelligence related activities. (JP 1-02)

close air support. Air action by fixed and rotary wing aircraft against hostile targets which are in close proximity to friendly forces and which require detailed integration of each air mission with the fire and movement of those forces. Also called **CAS.** (JP 1-02)

combat aviation advisory team. A special operations team specifically tailored to assess, advise, and train foreign aviation forces in air operations employment and sustainability. Teams support geographic combatant commanders throughout the operational continuum, primarily by facilitating the integration and interoperability of friendly and allied aviation forces supporting joint and multinational operations. Teams are specially trained and equipped to provide advisory assistance in the three interrelated areas of foreign internal defense

(FID), coalition support (CS), and unconventional warfare (UW). Also called **CAAT**. (AFDD 2-7)

Commander Air Force Special Operations Forces. The senior AFSOF Airman on the JFSOC or JSOTF chain of command. Also called **COMAFSOF**. (AFDD 2-7)

conventional forces. 1. Those forces capable of conducting operations using nonnuclear weapons. 2. Those forces other than designated special operations forces. (JP 1-02)

counterterrorism. Actions taken directly against terrorist networks and indirectly to influence and render global and regional environments inhospitable to terrorist networks Also called **CT.** (JP 1-02)

covert operation. An operation that is so planned and executed as to conceal the identity of or permit plausible denial by the sponsor. A covert operation differs from a clandestine operation in that emphasis is placed on concealment of the identity of sponsor rather than on concealment of the operation. (JP 1-02)

deception. Those measures designed to mislead the enemy by manipulation, distortion, or falsification of evidence to induce him to react in a manner prejudicial to his interests. (JP 1-02)

direct action. Short-duration strikes and other small-scale offensive actions conducted as a special operation in hostile, denied, or politically sensitive environments and which employ specialized military capabilities to seize, destroy, capture, exploit, recover, or damage designated targets. Direct action differs from conventional offensive actions in the level of physical and political risk, operational techniques, and the degree of discriminate and precise use of force to achieve specific objectives. Also called **DA.** (JP 1-02)

foreign internal defense. Participation by civilian and military agencies of a government in any of the action programs taken by another government or other designated organization to free and protect its society from subversion, lawlessness, and insurgency. Also called **FID.** (JP 1-02)

guerrilla force. A group of irregular, predominantly indigenous personnel organized along military lines to conduct military and paramilitary operations in enemy-held, hostile, or denied territory. (JP 1-02)

guerrilla warfare. Military and paramilitary operations conducted in enemy-held or hostile territory by irregular, predominantly indigenous forces. (JP 1-02)

infiltration. 1. The movement through or into an area or territory occupied by either friendly or enemy troops or organizations. The movement is made, either by small groups or by individuals, at extended or irregular intervals. When used in connection with the enemy, it infers that contact is avoided. 2. In intelligence usage, placing an agent or other person in a target area in hostile territory. Usually involves crossing a frontier or other guarded line. Methods of infiltration are: black (clandestine); gray (through legal crossing point but under false documentation); white (legal). (JP 1-02)

information operations. The integrated employment of the core capabilities of electronic warfare, computer network operations, psychological operations, military deception, and operations security, in concert with specified supporting and related capabilities, to influence, disrupt, corrupt or usurp adversarial human and automated decision making while protecting our own. Also called **IO.** (JP 1-02)

information superiority. That degree of dominance in the information domain, which permits the conduct of operations without effective opposition. (JP 1-02)

information warfare. Information operations conducted during time of crisis or conflict to achieve or promote specific objectives over a specific adversary or adversaries. Also called **IW.** (JP1-02)

insurgency. An organized movement aimed at the overthrow of a constituted government through use of subversion and armed conflict. (JP 1-02)

Intelligence, surveillance, and reconnaissance. An activity that synchronizes and integrates the planning and operation of sensors, assets, processing, exploitation, and dissemination systems in direct support of current and future operations. Also called **ISR.** (JP 1-02)

joint force commander. A general term applied to a combatant commander, subunified commander, or joint task force commander authorized to exercise combatant command (command authority) or operational control over a joint force. Also called **JFC.** (JP 1-02)

joint force special operations component commander. The commander within a unified command, subordinate unified command, or joint task force responsible to the establishing commander for making recommendations on the proper employment of assigned, attached, and/or made available for tasking special operations forces and assets; planning and coordinating special operations; or accomplishing such operational missions as may be assigned. The joint force special operations component commander is given the authority necessary to accomplish missions and tasks assigned by the establishing commander. Also called **JFSOCC.** (JP 1-02)

joint special operations air component commander. The commander within a joint force special operations command responsible for planning and executing joint special operations air activities. Also called **JSOACC.** (JP 1-02)

Joint special operations air detachment. The JSOAD is a tactical level C2 node composed of joint aviation units that normally is subordinate to a theater JFSOCC, JSOTF, or JSOACC depending on the size and duration of the operation.

joint special operations area. A restricted area of land, sea, and airspace assigned by a joint force commander to the commander of a joint special operations force to conduct special operations activities. The commander of joint special operations forces may further assign a specific area or sector within the joint special operations area to a subordinate commander for mission execution. The scope and duration of the special operations forces' mission, friendly and hostile situation, and politico-military considerations all influence the number, composition, and sequencing of special operations forces deployed into a joint special operations area. It may be limited in size to accommodate a discrete direct action mission or may be extensive enough to allow a continuing broad range of unconventional warfare operations. Also called **JSOA.** (JP 1-02)

joint special operations task force. A joint task force composed of special operations units from more than one Service, formed to carry out a specific special operation or prosecute special operations in support of a theater campaign or other operations. The joint special operations task force may have conventional nonspecial operations units assigned or attached to support the conduct of specific missions. Also called **JSOTF.** (JP 1-02)

multinational. Between two or more forces or agencies of two or more nations or coalition partners. (JP 1-02)

multinational operations. A collective term to describe military actions conducted by forces of two or more nations, typically organized within the structure of a coalition or alliance. (JP 1-02)

operational control. Command authority that may be exercised by commanders at any echelon at or below the level of combatant command. Operational control is inherent in combatant command (command authority) and may be delegated within the command. When forces are transferred between combatant commands, the command relationship the gaining commander will exercise (and the losing commander will relinquish) over these forces must be specified by the Secretary of Defense. Operational control is the authority to perform those functions of command over subordinate forces involving organizing and employing commands and forces, assigning tasks, designating objectives, and giving authoritative direction necessary to accomplish the mission. Operational control includes authoritative direction over all aspects of military operations and joint training necessary to accomplish missions assigned to the command. Operational control should be exercised through the commanders of subordinate organizations. Normally this authority is exercised through subordinate joint force commanders and Service and/or functional component commanders. Operational control normally provides full authority to organize commands and forces and to employ those forces as the commander in operational control considers necessary to accomplish assigned missions; it does not, in and of itself, include authoritative direction for logistics or matters of administration, discipline, internal organization, or unit training. Also called **OPCON.** (JP 1-02)

operations security. A process of identifying critical information and subsequently analyzing friendly actions attendant to military operations and other activities to: a. Identify those actions that can be observed by adversary intelligence systems. b. Determine indicators hostile intelligence systems might obtain that could be interpreted or pieced together to derive critical information in time to be useful to adversaries. c. Select and execute measures that eliminate or reduce to an acceptable level the vulnerabilities of friendly actions to adversary exploitation. Also called **OPSEC.** (JP 1-02)

overt operation. An operation conducted openly, without concealment. See also clandestine operation; covert operation. (JP 1-02)

psychological operations. Planned operations to convey selected information and indicators to foreign audiences to influence their emotions, motives, objective reasoning, and ultimately the behavior of foreign governments, organizations, groups, and individuals. The purpose of psychological operations is to induce or reinforce foreign attitudes and behavior favorable to the originator's objectives. Also called **PSYOP.** (JP I-02)

special forces. US Army forces organized, trained, and equipped to conduct special operations with an emphasis on unconventional warfare capabilities. Also called **SF.** (JP 1-02)

special operations. Operations conducted by specially organized, trained, and equipped military and paramilitary forces to achieve military, political, economic, or psychological objectives by unconventional military means in hostile, denied, or politically sensitive areas. These operations are conducted across the full range of military operations, independently or in coordination with operations of conventional, nonspecial operations forces. Political-military considerations frequently shape special operations, requiring clandestine, covert, or low visibility techniques and oversight at the national level. Special operations often differ from conventional operations in degree of physical and political risk, operational techniques, mode of employment, independence from friendly support, and dependence on detailed operational intelligence and indigenous assets. Also called **SO.** (JP 1-02)

special operations command. A subordinate unified or other joint command established by a joint force commander to plan, coordinate, conduct, and support joint special operations within the joint force commander's assigned area of operations. Also called **SOC**. (JP 1-02)

special operations expeditionary group. An independent group, normally the lowest command echelon of forces reporting directly to a COMAFFOR, JSOTF, JSOACC, or JTF. Also called **SOEG**. (AFDD 2-7)

special operations expeditionary squadron. The squadron is the basic fighting unit of the US Air Force. Squadrons are configured to deploy in support of crisis action requirements. However, an individual squadron is not designed to conduct independent operations; it requires support from other units to obtain the synergy needed for sustainable, effective operations. As such, an individual squadron or squadron element should not be presented by itself without provision for appropriate support and command elements. If a single operational squadron or squadron element is all that is needed to provide the desired operational effect it should deploy with provision for commensurate support and command and control elements. This squadron is normally subordinate to a special operations expeditionary group or wing. Also called **SOES**. (AFDD 2-7)

special operations expeditionary wing. Normally composed of a special operations wing or a wing slice. The SOEW is composed of the wing command element and appropriate groups. It is attached to a COMAFFOR, JSOTF, JSOACC, or JTF depending upon size, duration, and nature of the operation. The SOEW may be composed of units from different wings, but where possible, is formed from units of a single wing. Also called **SOEW**. (AFDD 2-7)

special operations forces. Those active and Reserve component forces of the military Services designated by the Secretary of Defense and specifically organized, trained, and equipped to conduct and support special operations. Also called **SOF**. (JP 1-02)

special operations liaison element. A special operations liaison team provided by the JFSOCC to the JFACC (if designated) to coordinate, deconflict, and integrate special operations air and surface operations with conventional air. Also called **SOLE**. (JP 1-02)

special operations weather team. A task-organized team of Air Force personnel organized, trained, and equipped to collect critical weather observations from data-sparse areas. These teams are trained to operate independently in permissive or uncertain environments, or as augmentation to other special operations elements in hostile environments, in direct support of special operations. Also called **SOWT**. (JP 1-02)

special reconnaissance. Reconnaissance and surveillance actions conducted as a special operation in hostile, denied, or politically sensitive environments to collect or verify information of strategic or operational significance, employing military capabilities not normally found in conventional forces. These actions provide an additive capability for commanders and supplement other conventional reconnaissance and surveillance actions. Also called **SR.** (JP 1-02)

special tactics team. A task-organized element of special tactics that may include combat control, pararescue, and combat weather personnel. Functions include austere airfield and assault zone reconnaissance, surveillance, establishment, and terminal control; terminal attack control; combat search and rescue; combat casualty care and evacuation staging; and tactical weather observations and forecasting. Also called **STT.** (JP 1-02) [Combat weather terminology has been changed to special operations weather.] [AFDD 2-7—joint publications have yet to be updated] {Words in brackets apply only to the US Air Force and are offered for clarity.}

tactical control. Command authority over assigned or attached forces or commands, or military capability or forces made available for tasking, that is limited to the detailed direction and control of movements or maneuvers within the operational area necessary to accomplish missions or tasks assigned. Tactical control is inherent in operational control. Tactical control may be delegated to, and exercised at any level at or below the level of combatant command. When forces are transferred between combatant commands, the command relationship the gaining commander will exercise (and the losing commander will relinquish) over these forces must be specified by the Secretary of Defense. Tactical control provides sufficient authority for controlling and directing the application of force or tactical use of combat support assets within the assigned mission or task. Also called **TACON.** (JP 1-02)

terrorism. The calculated use of unlawful violence or threat of unlawful violence to inculcate fear intended to coerce or to intimidate governments or societies in the pursuit of goals that are generally political, religious, or ideological. (JP 1-02)

unconventional warfare. A broad spectrum of military and paramilitary operations, normally of long duration, predominantly conducted through, with, or by indigenous or surrogate forces who are organized, trained, equipped, supported, and directed in varying degrees by an external source. It includes, but is not limited to, guerrilla warfare, subversion, sabotage, intelligence activities, and unconventional assisted recovery. Also called **UW.** (JP 1-02)